AUSTRALIA FACES SOUTHEAST ASIA

AMRY & MARY BELLE VANDENBOSCH

AUSTRALIA

FACES

SOUTHEAST

ASIA

The Emergence of a Foreign Policy

UNIVERSITY OF KENTUCKY PRESS

LEXINGTON 1967

PREFACE

For several centuries before World War II, Southeast Asia had been a calm backwater in world politics. With the Japanese occupation of Indochina in 1940 the attention of the world suddenly was drawn to the region. After the sweeping invasion by the Japanese after Pearl Harbor, and especially after the fall of Singapore in February, 1942, Southeast Asia became one of the most critical areas of the war. Japan's surrender did not bring peace and calm to the region, as colonial wars and Communist guerrilla activities followed the Japanese capitulation. Except for a few fragments of the Portuguese empire, western colonialism has disappeared from the region, except for East New Guinea, which is administered by Australia. The life of the new states has been turbulent, and they have experienced disorders, insurgency, and military takeovers. Nor has the region enjoyed international peace; there has been bitter and protracted conflict between great powers in this strategic corner of the world, as well as "confrontations" which came near to an outbreak of war.

No country was more affected by these changes and developments than Australia, a country settled primarily by westerners and situated on the edge of the explosive region. The changed situation profoundly influenced Australian national life. With the fall of Singapore, Australia suddenly had to readjust its foreign policy which psychologically was not easy. The pressure of current events forced it to move further in new directions. Developments in Southeast Asia are important for world peace; for Australia they may involve national survival, making its policy toward the region greatly important. Because of the close relations which have developed between the United States and Australia and the

United States' deep involvement in the region, Australian policy toward Southeast Asia should be of keen interest to Americans.

In this study we have quoted extensively from speeches in Australia's Parliament, official documents, and newspapers to give the reader the Australian point of view.

We incurred numerous debts of gratitude in making this study. The Commonwealth Institute of the University of London generously put its facilities at our disposal, and its staff members were very helpful. Sir Alan Watt and his staff at the Australian Institute of International Studies at Canberra extended us every courtesy. To these and others too numerous to mention we are deeply grateful.

May, 1967   AMRY VANDENBOSCH
                                        MARY BELLE VANDENBOSCH

CONTENTS

1 *Postwar Reappraisal of External Policy*

Situated as we are in the South-West corner of the Pacific, with the outlying islands of the Asian continent almost touching our own territories of New Guinea and Papua, our first and constant interest must be the security of our own home-land and the maintenance of peace in the area in which our country is geographically placed. We could many years ago reasonably regard ourselves as isolated from the main threats to our national security. and our traditional British Commonwealth and United States of issue because changes since the war have resulted in a shifting of potential aggression from the European to the Asian area, and our traditional British Commonwealth and United States of America friends have not yet completed their adjustments to the new situation. A very great burden of responsibility rests especially on us, but also upon the other British Commonwealth countries of this area.

. . .

It is indisputably true, . . . that peace is indivisible and that what takes place in any part of the world concerns us. But it should at all times be stressed that here in this part of the world we are faced with special problems, and it is to a solution of these problems that our attention should primarily be directed.

P. C. SPENDER
Minister for External Affairs
March 9, 1950.

THE SECOND WORLD WAR brought profound changes in Australia's relations with the world, and Australians have found agonizing their experience in reappraising their position and developing a foreign policy to meet unprecedented challenges. Australia's changed situation resulted chiefly from two developments. First, the neighboring region of Southeast Asia, which for several centuries had been a calm, inconspicuous region of the world, suddenly was drawn into the vortex of international politics by the Japanese invasion. Although Japan was ultimately defeated, a new threat to Southeast Asia and Australia emerged on the mainland of East Asia. Nor was the expulsion of Japan from the region followed by peace and quiet, but by strife. Minister for External Affairs Richard G. Casey summarized the new perils succinctly: "Instead of living in a tranquil corner of the globe we are now on the verge of the most unsettled region of the world."[1]

This change in conditions in Southeast Asia was worsened by the realization that Britain, on whom Australia had relied for its security, had proved unable to aid her dominion when it was threatened with an invasion by the triumphant Japanese armed forces. Unfortunately, Britain's military decline was not to be temporary. While recovering its former colonial territories, the United Kingdom soon adopted a policy of liquidating its imperial interests and reducing its military commitments, especially in that part of the world.

Australians were quite unprepared for the task of reorienting their foreign policy. In contrast with the thirteen English colonies in North America each of the Australian states remained a separate British colony until the proclama-

[1] In Parliament, Oct. 27, 1954. *Commonwealth Parliamentary Debates,* House, XV, 2382. "Unarguable facts of geography place Australia in a most dangerous and unstable part of the world." *Canberra Times,* Dec. 31, 1962.

tion of the commonwealth on January 1, 1901. Consequently, there developed no independent spirit, for Australia, as a Labor member of Parliament says, "grew up under the physical and psychological wing of Great Britain."[2] A number of factors contributed to this strong and continued British orientation. Australia was a white outpost in an out-of-the-way corner of the world, with a handful of Britishers[3] occupying a continent bounded by the vastness of the Indian and Pacific oceans. With such great resources to exploit they developed a high level of living, even by western standards. A strong trade union movement and vigorous Labor party politics insured the diffusion of prosperity. What caused Australians some anxiety was the thought either of foreign conquest, especially by an Asian power, or of large-scale Asian immigration. Since they were so few in numbers and so underdeveloped industrially, they could not possibly defend themselves against attack by a major power. Their living levels might be depressed and English culture submerged by the movement of numerous people from the populous and impoverished Asian countries to Australia.

Australia's response to this double threat was the promotion of British (and later of western and southern European) immigration, the exclusion of orientals (the "white Australia" policy), and the maintenance of close ties with the British Empire. So long as Britain ruled the sea, Australians felt reasonably safe, but Japan's rapid modernization and increasing world power concerned Australians and increased rather than diminished their reliance upon Britain. Other factors, such as the importance of the United Kingdom as a market for Australian products and Australia's dependence upon British capital for development, reinforced this strong pro-British orientation. The United Kingdom, which takes about one-fifth of the Australian exports and supplies some-

[2] J. F. Cairns, *Living With Asia* (Melbourne, 1965), 1.
[3] Australia's population was 3,765,000 in 1900; 5,411,000 in 1920; 7,069,000 in 1940; and was estimated at 11,360,000 in June, 1966.

what less than one-third of its imports, is Australia's most important trading partner.

The degree of favor for the British has varied among Australia's political parties, and it has been less strong with the Labor party, which has advocated a more independent and nationalist line. The Labor party was in power when World War I broke out, and it strongly supported Britain in the war. However, the party members split on the issue of conscription for overseas service.[4]

Despite the relative decline in British strength and prestige, Australia's attachment to the British and the Commonwealth diminished only slowly after World War II. More than a decade after the war an Australian specialist on his country's foreign policy could write: "The maintenance of strong links with Britain and the Commonwealth is an article of faith which is not today questioned by any of the political parties. . . . This firm adherence is the product both of emotion and rational judgment."[5] Also, the reasons for this attachment differ with the parties, and with the Labor party the desire to avoid too great a dependence upon the United States is an important factor.

The fall of Singapore in February, 1942, and the sinking of the British battleships, the *Prince of Wales* and the *Repulse*, was a traumatic experience for the Australian people and marks a sharp turning point in their history. These events produced a near-panic, causing Prime Minister John Curtin to exclaim that Australia now looked to America "free of any pangs as to our traditional links with the United Kingdom."[6] It was under these tragic circumstances that the new orientation of external policy emerged. During the first four decades of the federation, Australian foreign policy

[4] W. M. Hughes broke with the party on this issue in 1917 and with his followers joined the opposition to form a new government with himself as prime minister.
[5] Gordon Greenwood, "The Commonwealth," in *Australia in World Affairs, 1950-1955* (Melbourne, 1957), 89.
[6] Winston Churchill, *The Second World War* (Boston, 1950), IV, 8.

was passive; Australian foreign policy was British foreign policy. The fall of Singapore and the threat of Japanese invasion at a time when England was threatened with a German invasion brought an abrupt change. No longer able to depend on Britain, Australia suddenly was forced to look to the United States for its security and survival.

The Labor party was in power during this crisis. Prime Minister John Curtin and Minister for External Affairs Herbert Vere Evatt, who continued in office under Prime Minister J. B. Chifley, made a strong effort to develop an independent, forceful role for Australia in world politics. Evatt was concerned with the forming of a strong United Nations and an effective Australian participation in that organization as a middle power. His more pressing and immediate problem, however, was Southeast Asia, and he wanted to create a regional organization to treat security and other problems related to the Southwest Pacific.

With the coming to power of the Liberal-Country coalition at the end of 1949, Australia entered a new phase in the development of its foreign policy. This came about not so much because of the change of government, as by several other factors. Indonesia became independent and Australia acquired a populous Asian state as a close neighbor, the Communists drove the National government from the mainland of China, and the world had become deeply divided by the cold war. Moreover, with Great Britain beginning to liquidate the Empire, the old Commonwealth, composed of European peoples or countries dominated by them, was changing into a new association of many races with widely differing interests and hence with little unity. So only to the United States could Australia look for national security. Australia joined the Southeast Asia Treaty Organization, entered into a defense alliance with the United States, and generally moved steadily closer to the United States, supporting United States Asian and Pacific policies to the point of committing combat troops to Vietnam.

During the quarter of a century since the fall of Singapore, Australia departed substantially from its traditional ties. Sir Robert Menzies, who previously had been an ardent supporter of the Commonwealth, declared regretfully in 1962 that "for most of its members, the association is, in a sense, functional and occasional. The old hopes of concerting common policies are gone."[7] British leaders were beginning to feel the same way. British Prime Minister Sir Alec Douglas-Home was quoted as saying, "The Commonwealth is not a center of power. If, as is certain, power is to lie in Europe, then I think it is there that Britain ought to be."[8] There are at present indications that the Wilson government is becoming disillusioned with the Commonwealth and weary of the attacks it has had to endure from the African members because of Rhodesia and South Africa. Britain is asked to "take all the action and make all the sacrifices." Although most members of the Commonwealth expect Britain to support their policies, few give Britain any help with hers, and the British are beginning to doubt whether the economic advantages are worth the political and military burdens of the Commonwealth.[9] It is as if the United Kingdom, having freed nearly all of its colonies, at last demands freedom for itself. Should the United Kingdom obtain membership in the European Economic Community, the Commonwealth would be further weakened, though conceivably, if the "new" Commonwealth were dissolved, the "old" one might be renewed.

Factors other than security considerations also tend to weaken Australian-British ties. In Australian trade the United Kingdom is falling behind other countries, and Japan is about to overtake Britain as Australia's best customer. In the fiscal year ending June 30, 1966, Japan bought goods worth $527,968,000 and Britain $531,552,000; the previous

[7] *Current Notes*, XXXIII, 35.
[8] C. L. Sulzberger in *The New York Times*, March 25, 1966.
[9] Drew Middleton, *The New York Times*, Oct. 2, 1966.

year the figures were $493,584,000 and $578,144,000, respectively.[10] In the same years Japanese exports to Australia increased from $289,632,000 to $314,496,000, making Japan Australia's third biggest supplier, after Britain, $905,968,000, and the United States, $843,696,000. Britain now takes less than one-fifth of Australia's exports, whereas before the war it took more than one-half. Southeast Asia, with New Zealand and Japan, now takes about 42 percent of Australia's exports compared with 17 percent before the war. In the fiscal year ending June 30, 1966, Australian exports totaled $3,053,120,000, and imports were $3,291,232,000. Investments show much the same pattern. Since World War II much non-British capital has been invested in Australia, and with investments of about one billion dollars, the United States now probably has passed Britain as the largest foreign investor in the country.[11] Another factor is the rapidly changing economy of Australia. While it is not yet an industrialized country—only 14 percent of its exports are factory made—it is making great strides in this direction.[12] In the decade from 1954 to 1964, Australia's exports rose in volume by more than 80 percent, and it had become the twelfth ranking nation in world exports. Between 1960 and 1964 its exports of manufactures have almost doubled, and vast new mineral resources have been discovered.[13] Its population is growing at the rate of more than 2 percent annually. Such rapid economic development tends to reduce the dependence upon Britain and to produce a more independent spirit.

The increased volume and changing composition of immi-

[10] Australia changed to a decimal currency system on Feb. 14, 1966, at the rate of two dollars for a pound. At the early 1967 exchange rate, the Australian dollar equaled 1.12 U.S. dollars.

[11] About one-fourth of the $2.2 billion annual investment in Australian industry comes from abroad.

[12] See "Australia's Place Between Two Worlds," *The Times* (London), July 11, 1966.

[13] See *The Economist*, Nov. 20, 1965, CCVII, 863-64.

gration since World War II are modifying the national character and are having an influence in reorienting foreign policy. Until 1938 only immigration of persons from Britain was encouraged and few non-British settled in Australia. In 1947, Australia adopted the policy of assisting immigrants, and persons from all Europe were welcomed. From October, 1945, to March, 1960, more than one and one-half million immigrants came to Australia, with less than half from the United Kingdom.[14]

The introduction of so large a proportion of non-British persons into Australian society is certain eventually to influence the Australian attitude toward Britain and the Commonwealth. The non-British immigrants become loyal Australians, but they have little special sentiment for Britain. To a lesser degree, the tendency toward a more distinctly Australian orientation may be expected among the generation born in Australia, regardless of family origin. Few of the younger generation have sentimental qualms about drifting away from Britain. The shift from the pound to the dollar represents something more than currency reform. A former minister of immigration has suggested that the impact of the European settlers will strengthen Australian ties with the United States, because America has a favorable image with most Europeans, but that it will retard the growing Australian consciousness of Asia, because their attitudes will be Europe-centered for some time.[15]

There is a new Australia, with a new orientation, facing a new power relationship in Asia. As a western people living

[14] The total number of immigrants for the fifteen years was 1,544,994, with nearly 742,000 coming from the United Kingdom. The country-origin of the others was: Italy, 204,000; Netherlands, 116,295; Poland, 76,000; Germany, 75,300; Greece, 33,000; Yugoslavia, 27,000; Hungary, 20,000; Latvia, 20,000; Austria, 18,000; Czechoslovakia, 12,000. Figures given by Minister of Immigration A. R. Downer in *The Influence of Migration on Australian Foreign Policy*, Roy Milne Lecture, 1960, Australian Institute for International Affairs.
[15] Milne Lecture, 1960.

in an unstable Asian region, with a populous, unstable oriental state for a near neighbor, Australians understandably are concerned about their security. The tense situation in Southeast Asia presents Australia with problems enough, but beyond is the Asian giant, China, which includes one-fourth of the human race and occupies a strategic corner of the world. While Australians do not discount the dangers in Southeast Asia, they are worried more about a Chinese advance into the region, with Australia as its ultimate goal.

2 Domestic Politics and Foreign Policy

We should seek to erect a constitutional edifice which shall be a guarantee of liberty and union for all time to come, to the whole people of this continent and the adjacent islands, to which they shall learn to look up with reverence and regard, which shall stand strong as a fortress and be held sacred as a shrine.

ALFRED DEAKIN
1891

Australia is a middle power in more senses than one. It is clearly one in the general sense in which the expression is used. But also it has common interests with both the advanced and the underdeveloped countries; it stands in point of realized wealth between the haves and the have-nots. It is at the one time a granary and a highly industrialized country. It has a European background and is set in intimate geographical propinquity to Asia.

This ambivalence brings some strength and offers promise of a future of which Australia can be confident, a future of increasing influence. But it poses continuing problems in identifying peculiarly Australian objectives and in finding balance in the policies devised to obtain them.

SIR GARFIELD BARWICK
Minister for External Affairs
House of Representatives
March 11, 1964

APPARENTLY, WORLD POLITICS had a considerable influence on the Australian federation movement. Imperialist interests and movements in the Southwest Pacific helped to provide the impetus for union. The Australian colonists saw "little to unite for and nothing to unite against" until western powers established control over neighboring islands; union then became "a condition of survival to Australians."[1] External pressure, chiefly that arising from the German interest in New Guinea, led to the establishment in 1885 of a Federal Council, an organ of very limited functions comparable to the confederation formed by the American colonies in 1781. New Zealand and Fiji had aided in its founding, but New Zealand never joined it and Fiji's active participation in it was very brief. The Federal Council served as a halfway house to full federation in 1901, but without New Zealand and Fiji.[2]

Australian politics largely have been a contest between Labor and anti-Labor parties. The first country to have a Labor government, Australia has found its Labor party a consistent political force. In power during seven of the first sixteen years of the commonwealth and holding the balance of power in the other nine, the Labor party again was in office from 1929 to 1931 and from 1941 to 1949. It stood for a "socialism without dogma" and lived in isolation from socialist parties in other countries. Ironically, this party of isolationist and pacifist leanings bore the responsibility of government most of the time during the two World Wars.

Among the parties in opposition to Labor there is none whose history goes back to the beginning of the federation. The non-Labor parties frequently regrouped under various names. The present non-Labor parties are the Liberal and

[1] A. Wyatt Tilby, *Australia, 1688-1911* (Boston, 1912), 208.
[2] See L. F. Crisp, *Australian National Government* (Croydon, 1965), 5ff. for a good, brief account of the forces that led to federation.

Country parties, and a coalition of these has governed the country since 1949. One visible evidence of their strong pro-British orientation is the practice of the non-Labor parties when in control of the states still to appoint Englishmen as governors. Lord Casey was the first Australian-born governor-general appointed by a non-Labor government (1965). There had been two Australian-born governors-general before him.

The non-Labor parties were ardent supporters of the British Empire. The United Australian party, in power from 1932 to 1939, ignored the Statute of Westminster (which limited the British legislative powers) and made no attempts to enter into diplomatic relations with countries outside the British Commonwealth. Under the circumstances there was little need of a department of foreign affairs. The Department of External Affairs was set up in 1901, but it dealt only with Australian-United Kingdom relations, the administration of Papua, immigration, and such matters. It was abolished in 1916 and reestablished in 1921 to deal with League of Nations matters. It was under the direction of the secretary of the Prime Minister's Department. In 1935 it became an independent department, but it was not until 1940 that direct diplomatic representations were exchanged with foreign countries.[3]

The attitude of the non-Labor parties before World War II toward foreign policy was clearly revealed in the Italo-Ethiopian conflict in 1935. When the question of the application of sanctions against Italy after its invasion of Ethiopia came before the League of Nations in 1935, the Australian government supported the League's action not on the grounds of collective security but out of loyalty to Britain. The attitude of the government of those years was expressed

[3] In June, 1946, the personnel, at home and abroad, of the Department of External Affairs numbered only 410; by June, 1966, it had increased to 1,570. More than half of Australia's diplomatic representatives are now stationed in Asia.

graphically by Prime Minister Lyons' phrase, "tune in to Britain." When war broke out in Europe in September, 1939, the government announced that since Britain was at war, Australia was also. There was no debate.[4] The attitudes of the leaders of the non-Labor parties are revealed by some of their statements. Sir Earle Page, a leader of the Country party, once said, "either we are in the British Empire or we turn aside upon some lonely road of our own never knowing where it will take us."[5] Robert G. Menzies, leader of the Liberal party and prime minister in 1939-1941 and 1949-1966, was an eloquent champion of the Empire. He favored a single, unified foreign policy for the entire British Empire, and he feared what would happen if the dominions pursued independent foreign policies, saying it could lead only to "British division and defeat." He hoped to see an imperial conference not only of prime ministers but of farmers and manufacturers. "I believe that, if we are to be restored as an Empire in a restored world, then our first collaboration must be within our own family of nations."[6] Harold Holt, the current leader of the Liberal party and prime minister since Menzies' retirement in January, 1966, in the debate on the ANZAC agreement of 1944, spoke of "the almost mystical tie which exists between us" members of the Empire and was critical of the pact, because it tended "to weaken the strength of the whole."[7]

Sir Percy Spender, minister for external affairs, said much

[4] This was in striking contrast with South Africa where war was declared only after a bitter debate and a neutrality resolution was defeated by a narrow margin, and with Canada where the government delayed the proclamation of war for several days in order to demonstrate that it was not automatic but a free act of an independent country.

When the Japanese struck Pearl Harbor on Dec. 7, 1941, the Labor Party, with Curtin as prime minister, declared war on Japan, and at once, several hours before the United Kingdom government did.

[5] Quoted by Peter Coleman in Peter Coleman and others, *Forces in Australian Politics* (Melbourne, 1963), 6.

[6] July 18, 1944, *Commonwealth Parliamentary Debates*, House, CLXXIX, 106.

[7] July 20, 1944, *CPD*, House, CLXXIX, 313-14.

the same thing in 1950 but less emotionally and with some indication of the implications of this orientation:

Since the head and corner of the British Commonwealth is the United Kingdom, and since our security is to a large extent dependent upon her strength and influence in world affairs, we must be vitally concerned in her interests and safety. Next, therefore, to the maintenance of peace in the Pacific, and almost coincidental with it comes our interest in the maintenance of peace and security in Western Europe. . . . We also have a special interest in and duty to the British Commonwealth and to each of its members. It must be a constant purpose of Australian foreign policy to strengthen the different ties which exist between us and to build up and not to weaken our composite power and influence for peace.[8]

He saw that the Commonwealth under the impact of the forces of nationalism and internationalism had undergone fundamental changes during the previous decade, making necessary a new approach to all questions which might affect it.

Imperial unity and national freedom, however, were incompatible. The Liberal and Country leaders seemed willing to sacrifice independence for imperial unity, but how long they could or would have adhered to this position can only be speculated. In any case, as the membership of the Commonwealth extended beyond the original white or white-controlled dominions, the ideal became progressively diluted until it ceased to have much content or meaning. Moreover, beginning with the fall of Singapore, the Empire loyalists suffered a number of rude shocks, and the Liberal and Country party leaders had to adjust their thinking and their policies to the altered conditions. As early as 1947, Menzies, then the leader of the opposition in Parliament, said "our foreign relations become increasingly important to us as our isolation from the centre of the British Empire becomes

[8] March 9, 1950, *CPD*, House, CCVI, 154-55.

more marked."[9] This amounted to saying that the Empire had weakened and that Australia no longer could look to it for protection. The Menzies government supported the United Kingdom in the Suez crisis of 1956, but it also joined SEATO (South East Asia Treaty Organization), and it entered into an alliance with the United States (ANZUS— Australian, New Zealand, United States Defense Treaty) from which the United Kingdom was excluded.

In two decades after World War II, Labor and non-Labor partisans reversed almost completely their positions on Australian relations with Britain and the Commonwealth, on the one hand, and the United States, on the other. In the political campaign of 1946, Laborites emphasized the role of the United States in repelling the Japanese attack and Australia's salvation by the American naval victory in the Coral Sea, expressing their gratitude to the United States for its firm defense of Australia. Labor leaders pointed out that it was a Labor government that turned to the United States for help in Australia's hour of desperate need. By contrast, the Liberals deemphasized this and stressed loyalty to Britain, the Empire, and the Commonwealth. By the 1966 campaign the two parties had reversed their positions and were more extreme in their stands. The Liberals not only ardently supported the American alliance and the United States policy in Vietnam, but also made cooperation with President Johnson their theme, opening themselves to the opposition's charge of "lap-dog acceptance of L.B.J.'s every attitude." Labor, especially its leader, A. A. Calwell, took an increasingly extreme anti-American position.

THE FEDERAL ASPECTS of the constitutional system of Australia are modeled after those of the United States. Because the country's sparse population is spread over a vast territory

[9] Feb. 26, 1947, *CPD*, House, CXC, 852.

with a large, practically unpopulated, geographic area at the center, life remains decentralized. Primary interest remains at the state level. The states are large in area: Western Australia covers nearly 1,000,000 square miles, and Queensland has 667,000. The smallest, Tasmania, is somewhat isolated as an island. Moreover, the life of each state is dominated by a large city; more than half the population of the commonwealth lives in the six state capitals. All of this tends to make the commonwealth a federation of city states. Few persons have any real national standing, and until 1964 there was no newspaper which attempted a national scope. As elsewhere, an increasing concentration of ownership of news media has taken place.[10]

Australia represents a strange political anomaly. While its people desire a highly developed welfare state, its constitution does not give the commonwealth government power to enact sufficient social and economic controls to bring it about, and obviously the states separately cannot create a broad socialization of economic life. The people have been reluctant to increase the power of the central government, as the defeat of numerous proposals to amend the constitution has shown. As in the United States, the courts have given a very liberal interpretation of the defense powers of the federal government. In wartime the activities and control of the commonwealth government are expanded tremendously, but when the war is over, much of this power must be relinquished. During World War II the Labor government made a vigorous drive for a constitutional revision which would have given the commonwealth Parliament ample power to make laws "for carrying into effect the war aims and objects of Australia as one of the United Nations, including the attainment of economic security and social

[10] See "The Mass Media" in *Australian Society: A Sociological Introduction,* ed. A. F. Davies and S. Encel (Melbourne, 1965). The new national newspaper is *The Australian* published at Canberra.

justice in the postwar world, and for the purpose of postwar reconstruction," but the drive failed.[11]

Although all parties have at times been interested in amending the constitution to increase the power of the commonwealth government, the Labor party most consistently has sought reform. Yet while the Labor party seeks the nationalization of political power (and boasts of its long record of struggle for democracy), its organizational structure favors minority control. The Federal Conference, which meets biennially, and the Federal Executive, which meets twice a year, are composed of an equal number of delegates from each state—six for the Conference and two for the Executive. Tasmania, with less than one-tenth of the population of New South Wales, has the same number of delegates as New South Wales in both bodies. New South Wales and Victoria together have about two-thirds of the country's population, yet the Labor party organization can be controlled by the other four states. This is all the more significant because the Conference and the Federal Executive exercise a close control over the Labor members of Parliament and Labor governments.

The power of the Conference and of the Federal Executive has become a political liability for the Labor party. The issue was involved in the 1963 campaign when the Liberals warned the country against a Labor government which would be the "hired lackeys of thirty-six outsiders."[12] The image of "thirty-six faceless men" increasingly has become a political burden for the Laborites. Some change in the structure of the Labor party organization may be expected.

[11] See Kenneth Hamilton Bailey, "The Constitution and Its Problems," *Australia* (Berkeley, 1947); L. F. Crisp, *The Australian Federal Labor Party, 1901-1951* (London, 1955), Ch. XII, "Labor and the Commonwealth Constitution."

[12] The issue arose over the proposed establishment of United States nuclear bases in Australia. There was doubt whether the Federal Conference would endorse the position of Labor leader Calwell and his deputy E. G. Whitlam, who favored the bases.

3 Herbert Vere Evatt and Labor Nationalism

The time has come to speak frankly and to declare that our two countries, as the two main centres of civilization in these two areas, have a special responsiiblity to discharge. Equally we have an undoubted right to speak, not only because our whole future— what the Prime Minister called "the life-and-death interest of Australia and New Zealand"—is involved but also because of the leading and resolute part the two countries have played ever since the outbreak of the present war in September, 1939.

We have not suggested that these territorial issues are for determination by Australia and New Zealand alone: we have stated temperately but frankly that all dispositions and changes should be made only with our concurrence and as part of a general Pacific settlement.

. . .

It is necessary to get rid once and for all of the idea that Australia's international status is not a reality, and that we are to remain adolescent forever.

HERBERT VERE EVATT
Minister for External Affairs
House of Representatives
Feb. 10 and July 20, 1944.

THOUGH AUSTRALIA HAD taken a noteworthy part in World War I, had made its voice heard strongly at the Paris Peace Conference, and had played an active role in the League of Nations, it was still largely passive in foreign policy when the Labor party came to power in 1941. That year a decided change took place. This change resulted from the juncture of four factors; a desperate global war, the decline of British power in Asia, the Labor party's rise to power, and the appointment of Dr. Herbert Vere Evatt as minister of external affairs. Evatt, an able and forceful political leader with decided views on foreign policy, pressed hard for a greater Australian participation in Allied councils which determined the conduct of the war in the Pacific, and he demanded that his country's voice be heard in the making of peace settlements.

LONG BEFORE AUSTRALIANS could pursue their own foreign policy they had a keen interest in the disposition of the islands to the north of them and strongly pressured Britain to act.[1] Australians made demands for the annexation of New Guinea as early as 1867. When in the 1870's the Germans seemed interested in the islands of the Southwest Pacific, the premier of New South Wales urged the British government to annex them all. Such a measure would be "consistent with the maritime supremacy of England" and would "conduce much to the tranquility and peace of the Australian colonies." In the early 1880's, Sir Thomas McIlwraith argued that Australians must take New Guinea "for the purpose of keeping bad neighbors from coming near them." He warned that foreign acquisition of the territory south of the equator would be "highly detrimental to the

[1] See W. K. Hancock, *Australia* (London, 1930), 241-43.

safety and well-being of the British possessions and injurious to the interests of the Empire."[2]

Prime Minister Hughes fought hard at the Paris Peace Conference to strengthen his country's position in the region. Since Australian troops had wrested northeast New Guinea from the Germans, Hughes had fully expected that Australia's desire for outright annexation of the territory would be granted. He opposed bitterly the transfer of the German islands north of the equator to an "actual or potential" enemy of Australia.[3] Not surprisingly, he strongly opposed the Japanese demand for recognition of the principle of racial equality. Hughes was deeply disappointed in the results of the conference for his country. Australia did not acquire sovereignty over northeast New Guinea, but only the right to administer it as a mandated territory, and Japan obtained control of the German islands north of the equator, though only as a mandatory power. This so disturbed him that he proclaimed a Monroe Doctrine for the Australian region. "While the Monroe Doctrine exempts the two Americas from the jurisdiction of the League of Nations we would not allow anything relating to our sphere in the Pacific to be regarded as a proper subject for submission to the tribunal."[4]

EVATT UNDOUBTEDLY WAS the influential force behind the

---

[2] Hancock, *Australia*, 242.

[3] In May and June, 1918, Hughes visited the United States where he conferred with President Wilson and other political leaders. In a speech in New York he was in a sense prophetic about the future relations of Australia and the United States. He charged Germany with the intention of taking over the Australian continent. "This," he said, "brings me to a matter of life and death importance to Australia. The United States, Australia and New Zealand have common interests in the Pacific. And Australia looks to you, her elder brother, to stand by her around the conference table as well as on the field of battle. For if we are to continue to be a commonwealth of free people, we must have guarantees against enemy aggression in the future." *The New York Times*, June 1, 1918.

[4] Hancock, *Australia*, 243.

Australian-New Zealand agreement of 1944,[5] generally called the ANZAC agreement. The pact was a sharp diplomatic move by the two small states to warn the great powers, and especially the United States, not to ignore their rights and interests when they determined the terms of peace in the Southwest Pacific. Apparently, this move was caused by deep resentment at being left out of the discussions at the Cairo conference which issued the declaration on Allied objectives in the war against Japan.[6] Essentially, the ANZAC agreement was a move by the two countries to stake out their claims in the Southwest Pacific.

The agreement, which consisted of forty-four articles, covered much ground, and only the most important provisions can be summarized here. The two governments agreed to give "mutual assurances" that on matters of common interest they would exchange information and views, and they agreed that there "shall be the maximum degree of unity in the presentation elsewhere of the views of the two countries." They further agreed "to act together in matters of common concern in the Southwest and South Pacific areas."

The two governments agreed that they should have "representation at the highest level on all armistice planning and executive bodies" and that "as a matter of cardinal importance" they should both be associated in the membership and in the establishment of any international organization for the maintenance of peace and security. The most important article of the agreement called for a "regional zone of defence," comprising the Southwest and South Pacific areas, within the framework of a general system of world security. Also, they concurred that such a regional security

---

[5] Signed at Canberra, Jan. 21, 1944.
[6] The declaration made by President Roosevelt, Generalissimo Chiang Kai-shek, and Prime Minister Churchill on Dec. 1, 1943, stated that Japan would be stripped of all the territory it acquired since 1894.

zone "shall be established and that this zone shall be based on Australia and New Zealand, stretching through the arc of islands north and northeast of Australia to Western Samoa and the Cook Islands." Pending the establishment of a general security system, they agreed that it would be "proper" for Australia and New Zealand "to assume full responsibility for policing or sharing in policing" such areas in the region as might be agreed upon.

As might be expected, the two governments also commented upon the disposition of enemy territories in the Pacific. They declared that the interim administration and the ultimate disposition of these territories was of vital importance to them, that "any such disposal should be effected only with their agreement and as part of a general Pacific settlement," and that "no change in the sovereignty or system of control of any of the Pacific islands" should be made, "except as a result of an agreement to which they are parties or in the terms of which they have both concurred."

In other articles the governments proposed an international convention to regulate all air transport services, a world air transport authority to operate all international air trunk routes, and a South Seas regional commission to coordinate efforts to advance the welfare of the inhabitants of the various Pacific territories. In an agreement which contained so many provisions seeking greater international cooperation and control an article promising "one another full support in maintaining the accepted principle that every Government has the right to control immigration and emigration in regard to all territories within its jurisdiction" seems out of place, yet its inclusion is understandable and is of great importance to Australia and New Zealand.

The agreement was in treaty form, thus becoming the first treaty made by Australia. It was negotiated and signed with much publicity, no doubt intended to draw the world's attention. The agreement provided for its ratification by the governments, but not by the Parliaments of the two countries. There was, nevertheless, a warm debate about it in the Australian Parliament, where the treaty was criticized as typical of the isolationism which had controlled Labor party thinking for years. Australia and New Zealand had been very fortunate, it was said, in that they had developed under the protection of the British Empire. Unfortunately, the Empire, based mainly on the strength of Great Britain itself, could not in the future give the same protection that it had in the past. Even so, the help of Britain and the Empire would be even more necessary in the future. "Forces from the United States," Senator Philip A. McBride said, "are already engaged in preserving Australia's independence, and in the future we shall have to look more than ever to that great country for protection." This was not the time to "flaunt to the world our puny ideas of independence." Australia and New Zealand had said, in effect, that no changes must be made without their full concurrence. The agreement was "a definite affront to all those people we need now, and shall need to a degree quite as great in the future." North of Australia were countries with populations totaling more than a billion whose living standards were much lower than those of Australia and New Zealand. These peoples were land- and commodity-hungry, and if Australia had to rely solely upon its own power in its defense against them, it would be overwhelmed, Senator McBride argued.[7] Another senator feared the agreement would encourage isolationists in the United States.

Criticism of the agreement in the House of Representatives ran along the same lines. Its members said the agreement should first have been discussed at the Imperial Conference,

[7] March 15, 1944, *Commonwealth Parliamentary Debates*, Senate, CLXXVII, 1313-20.

which met just prior to the conclusion of the agreement. Moreover, it was concluded without reference to Parliament. John McEwen, the leader of the Country party, declared:

We have the spectacle of the Australian-New Zealand Agreement concluded at a time when the future developments in the Pacific theatre are in the melting pot. If we are to expect a fair discussion upon these subjects with our powerful friend, the United States of America, and if we expect the other Pacific nations to come along in good faith to discuss with us the settlement of the problems, surely they must expect us to come with free hands, untied by contracts; but we have made a contract. We have bound ourselves, as New Zealand has bound itself.[8]

Harold Holt, who two decades later was to succeed Menzies as leader of the Liberal party and prime minister, was critical of the agreement because it tended to give the world the impression that there were weaknesses in the imperial setup and a waning of allegiance to the Empire. "It is because I believe that Australia is going to exert great influence by maintaining an unbroken membership in the British Empire that I criticize the type of pact that we see in the Australia-New Zealand Agreement. However trivial it may be, we depart in that agreement to some extent from the principle of Imperial rule by emphasizing our separateness and our own individual problems; and we thereby tend to weaken the strength of the whole. That is a danger against which every Australian Government must guard."[9]

Evatt answered the attack with characteristic bluntness: "Whether or not one agrees with every clause of the Agreement, it is necessary to get rid once and for all of the idea that Australia's international status is not a reality, and that we are to remain adolescent forever. . . . The Government has no apologies to make for the agreement. I think it will

[8] July 18, 1944, *CPD*, House, CLXXVII, 229.
[9] July 20, 1944, *CPD*, House, CLXXVII, 313-14.

turn out to be an historic agreement." As the two great dominions which had to uphold British civilization in that part of the world, they had the duty to make "a positive contribution to the future of the Pacific." The agreement was not isolationist, he contended. "Nowhere in the agreement is it possible, on any honest reading, to find evidence of an isolationist approach or an attempt to exclude other powers from their proper position in the area. The whole agreement contemplates a regional arrangement which from beginning to end, is made subject to a system of world security."[10]

Evatt took advantage of the occasion to pacify the Americans, as well as to appear pro-American rather than anti-American, as his critics had charged. America had been offended by the agreement,[11] and American leaders were convinced that one of the treaty's primary objects was to notify the United States that no settlement should be made in the Southwest Pacific without the full concurrence of the two dominions. The statement in the pact that the use of a base in wartime does not "afford any basis for territorial claims or rights of sovereignty or control after the conclusion of hostilities" was rather pointed. After stating clearly that the agreement was not aimed at the United States and that relations with that country could not be more friendly, Evatt said, "Many unthinking people in Australia today show an inclination to undervalue the magnificent assistance which the United States of America has rendered to Australia, and without which we should not have been able to survive as a nation."[12]

An interesting appraisal of the agreement and the motives behind it was made by Paul Hasluck, who then was a staff member of the Ministry of External Affairs but who later

[10] July 19, 1944, *CPD*, House, CLXXVII, 229-35.
[11] The writer, at the time a member of the staff of the Department of State, remembers the excitement the agreement caused.
[12] July 19, 1944, *CPD*, House, CLXXVII, 238.

resigned because of inability to get along with Evatt. He was elected to Parliament in 1949 and became minister of external affairs in 1964, after having served as minister of territories and minister of defense. Hasluck believed that Evatt wanted to assert the dominant Australian interest in the South and Southwest Pacific and viewed the provisions of the agreement and some of Evatt's speeches as "unsolved confusion between the desire that Australia should take the lead in all things in the Southwest Pacific and the need to get someone to contribute the means for ensuring our security."[13]

Curtin viewed the agreement as a threefold landmark, namely, in the international collaboration in the Pacific, in the development of Australian and New Zealand foreign policy, and in the constitutional growth of the British Empire.[14] Nonpartisan appraisal was a bit more sober. The *Sydney Morning Herald* of January 24, 1944, both praised and questioned the pact. By pooling resources and coordinating policies Australia and New Zealand could provide the nucleus of a strong peacekeeping force in the South Pacific, but only if they were prepared to maintain a high level of armed strength. This would require a sharp break with prewar habits and tradition. Even then, with the war in the Pacific about at its climax a part of the armed forces of the country could not be used in a large part of the proposed regional defense zone. No matter how strong an armed force the two countries did develop, however, for security they still would have to rely primarily upon the United States and Britain. "That chastening reflection should make us wary of appearing too importunate in our claims or pretentious in our ambitions." The Canberra Conference

---

[13] "Australia and the Formation of the United Nations," *Royal Australian Historical Society, Journal and Proceedings*, XL, Part III, 1954. Hasluck added, "One was also aware of an almost psychological antipathy to any power that was greater than Australia." Evatt became more moderate in his views, Hasluck states.

[14] *Sydney Morning Herald*, Jan. 24, 1944.

"attempted too much too soon. The war has still to be won, and mainly by the Great Powers whose voices will be predominant in the settlement." The real value of the agreement was to be sought in the "identity of interest and the essential unity therein expressed. Our two countries have linked their destinies, and stand pledged to work in closest harmony for the peace and advancement of this area of the Pacific. This is a great and most promising achievement."

THE BASIC DIFFERENCE in the approach of the Labor party government from that of the non-Labor opposition was revealed by the discussion in Parliament of the negotiations with the United States for the use of the Manus Island base. The base, which had been constructed during the war by the United States at a cost of $150,000,000, was on an island which was part of the New Guinea mandated territory, thus not under Australian sovereignty, though this fact seems to have entered the negotiations hardly at all. The United States defense departments naturally wished to retain the use of bases they had built in the Southwest Pacific, but it is not clear exactly what the United States government requested—whether it wanted sovereignty over the base or the right to use it on a joint and reciprocal basis. Phases of the negotiations remain obscure.

The real debate, and it was a heated one, came in a somewhat posthumous fashion. The American request was most likely made in 1945, for Manus Island was one of the nine bases in the Pacific which, according to an August, 1945, report of the House Naval Affairs Subcommittee, the Navy Department insisted needed to be retained by the United States.[15] There was very little discussion of the matter at the time, chiefly because there was no reliable public infor-

[15] *The New York Times,* Sept. 6, 1945.

mation about the negotiations. There were a few exchanges on the floors of Parliament which revealed the attitudes of the government and the opposition, however. A member of the House, referring to press stories of the American request for Manus Island, said, "The more we can have the warp of America and the woof of Australia woven together in the fabric of southwest Pacific defence, the more secure will this country be and the greater will be the height to which we shall rise as a nation."[16] To this A. A. Calwell replied, "The honorable member who says that we have the right to give away territory which is administered by us under mandate, also says that we have no right at all to determine a foreign policy for Australia."[17]

The general view of the opposition members was that the government had done the country a great disservice by demanding the return of the base. Australian security was dependent upon close cooperation with the United States, and friendship with the United States should be fostered. Australia could not rely solely upon the United Nations to guarantee her security because of the disagreement among its members and the right of the veto by the great powers in the Security Council. British help was limited. New Zealand was a help, but it was not enough.

Evatt made some general statements in this debate, but he refused to divulge anything about the status of negotiations. Bases could not be dealt with piecemeal but had to be considered as part of overall defense arrangements for the Western Pacific. As for Manus Island, "the Government would not make an arrangement regardless of any understandings as to the uses to which such islands could be put in the event of a disturbance in the Pacific."[18] A short time before, he had told the House that the government would, enter into no commitments which would lessen Australian

---

[16] J. P. Abbott, March 26, 1946, *CPD*, House, CXXXVI, 604.
[17] *CPD*, House, CXXXVI, 608.
[18] *CPD*, House, CXXXVI, 629.

control over their territories. Joint use of installations on a reciprocal basis would be welcomed, but bases were only a part of a whole military plan for the defense of an area.[19] He was repeatedly pressed for information about the negotiations, but dodged by stating that the protracted negotiations still were in progress and that he would make a statement as soon as possible. A year later, in reply to queries, Evatt said that "negotiations . . . had reached a stage which made it impossible . . . to disclose any details."[20]

What Evatt was angling for as one possible solution to his problem probably was revealed in a speech at the National Press Club in Washington in November, 1945, when he said that Australia was prepared to grant another country the use of its military bases if that country would accept responsibility for the security of the area which the bases were designed to protect.[21]

In June, 1947, the minister for defense presented to Parliament the government's Five Year Defense Plan, which included a proposal to establish a naval base on Manus Island. The Australian government would welcome an arrangement for its joint use by the United States on the basis of reciprocity.[22] This led a senator to inquire whether this meant that the American request for the base had been rejected. A Labor senator retorted that the future of Manus and its development was a matter of high defense policy and this was no time to discuss it.[23]

It was not until the treaty of peace with Japan came before Parliament in February, 1952, that the Manus Island base negotiations were discussed at any length. The debate on the Japanese treaty naturally involved a discussion of Australian security. However, a year before, a leading

19 March 13, 1946, *CPD*, House, CXXXVI, 200.
20 March 19, 1947, *CPD*, House, CXC, 884.
21 *The New York Times*, Nov. 17, 1945.
22 June 4, 1947, *CPD*, Senate, CXCII 3339.
23 *CPD*, Senate, CXCII, 3464.

metropolitan newspaper had reopened the whole matter by an article, "The Scandal of Manus," apparently based upon diplomatic documents.[24] The deputy leader of the Labor party challenged Minister for External Affairs Casey to produce the papers showing that the Chifley government had refused a United States request for the Manus Island base.[25] Casey replied that he would not make the papers available, but said that America had asked for the use of the defense equipment and that the request was refused.[26]

In this debate there was a very sharp exchange between Casey, now minister for external affairs, and Evatt, who held the position at the time of the Manus Island base negotiations. Casey said that the United States government had asked merely for joint use of the base, while Evatt insisted that the Australian government had offered the use not only of Manus Island and its facilities but also of any other Australian bases outside or inside of Australia, but that the American government had requested far greater rights and on a nonreciprocal basis. For example, the United States at one point proposed an arrangement whereby, in the event of war in the Pacific in which the United States remained neutral, Australia would not have the right to use Manus Island, its own territory. This was unacceptable to the Chifley government. The United States was neutral for the first years of both World Wars and might be so again in another war in the Pacific, and thus Manus Island might be removed from Australian control. According to Evatt, the

[24] The *Sydney Morning Herald*, Jan. 21, 1951. Evatt charged the newspaper with "illegitimate use of confidential material passing between Governments." Feb. 28, 1952, *CPD*, House, CCXVI, 597.

[25] Feb. 27, 1952, *CPD*, House, CCXVI, 476.

[26] *CPD*, House, CCXVI, 485. Casey remarked that while the files were voluminous, they were not as complete as they should have been. There was no written record of many stages of the negotiations that were conducted orally. This statement might imply that Evatt, as minister for external affairs, had purposely left them incomplete. Evatt suggested that the papers might have been removed from the files at the time the article in the *Sydney Morning Herald* was written.

Australian government then decided that the negotiations should be continued by the British Commonwealth with the goal of forming a regional pact providing for mutual use of facilities, but the American representatives refused to talk with the Commonwealth as a group and insisted that negotiations be carried out on a bilateral basis.[27] The matter was placed before a Commonwealth Conference, composed of Australia, the United Kingdom, and New Zealand, but it is not clear whether Australia imposed its decision upon the conference or whether, as Evatt sometimes made it appear, the decision that there must be an overall agreement was more or less forced upon Australia. It is more likely that the others acquiesced in this demand because of Evatt's determination. Evatt said he had discussed with President Truman and his secretary of state the desirability of a regional pact providing for reciprocal use of bases, instead of considering an individual base such as Manus. "They were reasonable terms, and might have been agreed to except that the centre of gravity for the United States went much further north."[28] Evatt's critics, however, said that if Australia had accepted the American request, the American line of defense in the Pacific would have been drawn much wider and might even have included Malaya.[29]

Casey probably summarized the matter correctly. "He [Evatt] attempted to get a broad regional agreement in the Pacific with the United States of America. . . . That, if I may say so with great respect, was a perfectly justifiable thing to attempt. . . . He aimed too high. . . . The Americans cooled off."[30] However, a few alternate explanations are possible. The Australian and the United States governments did not agree about the meaning of reciprocity in this case.

27 The United States defense departments apparently were originally interested in nine bases in the Southwest Pacific situated in Australian, British, and French territories. *The New York Times*, Sept. 6, 1945.
28 Feb. 28, 1952, *CPD*, House, CCXVI, 598.
29 Feb. 28, 1952, *CPD*, House, CCXVI, 607.
30 Feb. 28, 1952, *CPD*, House, CCXVI, 746-47.

The United States had built the base on Manus Island at great cost, and it did not define reciprocity as having the right to use defense facilities which it had built in exchange for granting the Australians the right to use other American bases. As the Americans saw it, all reciprocity involved was Australia's right to build bases on American territory.

Also, American thinking likely contained an element of isolationism. The United States was uncertain about the degree of commitment it wished to make in the Southwest Pacific.[31] Australia has pushed the United States for a complete commitment for the defense of all the Southwest Pacific, all of Southeast Asia, and Australia. During the Malaysian confrontation Australia worried about what the United States would do if Indonesia should attack Australian forces in North Borneo with full strength and even attack Australian territory. In exchange for complete coverage by the United States the Liberal-Country government seems prepared to give the United States complete diplomatic support in the region. Evatt and the Chifley government, however, wanted an arrangement which would give Australia greater freedom of action and greater influence in world politics, and this was a primary objective of the Australian-New Zealand agreement of 1944. In the debate Evatt said that in its foreign policy Australia had to cooperate closely with the United Kingdom and the Commonwealth, and in the Pacific with the United States, but that Australia should not be a "satellite," always doing what the

[31] For a good but brief account and analysis of the Manus Island case see N. Rosecrance, *Australian Diplomacy and Japan, 1945-1951* (Melbourne, 1962). President Roosevelt had thought in terms of "international" bases as part of a system of collective security under the United Nations; the idea seems to have died with him. A congressional subcommittee reporting in Aug., 1945, held quite different views. "The maintenance of peace in the Pacific being primarily the responsibility of the United States, we must have the necessary authority." The subcommittee named the base on Manus Island as one of several in the Southwest Pacific to which the United States should demand full title. U.S. Congress, House, Committee on Naval Affairs, Subcommittee on Pacific Bases, *Study of Pacific Bases*, 79th Cong., 1st Sess., Aug. 6, 1945.

United States wanted it to do. It should not allow itself to become "merely an instrument of another's policy."[32] This is the basic criticism that the Labor party consistently has made about the foreign policies of the Menzies and Holt governments.

THE VIEW OF the Australian government toward the Indonesian movement for national independence was colored strongly by Labor ideology, but it also bore the influence of Evatt and, to a lesser degree, that of the Prime Minister, J. B. Chifley. Chifley generally supported independence movements not only because he believed these aspirations deserved support, but also because he was convinced that an attempt to reimpose European authority in Southeast Asia was "like drawing a stick through water" and would be futile.[33] Evatt strongly supported Labor's anticolonial sentiments and also was determined that Australia would assert a leading role in the affairs of Southeast Asia. As colonialism receded in the region, Australia's interests would increase and its influence would mount. "We must," he told Parliament in 1947, "work for a harmonious association of democratic states in the South-East Asia area, and see in the development of their political maturity opportunity for greatly increased living standards throughout the area." He advocated the establishment of regional commissions in the South Pacific and in Southeast Asia to promote the well-being of the region's peoples. Such organizations would "at least facilitate the free and rapid interchange of basic information concerning the problem of administration, education, health, agriculture, commerce and cultural relations."[34]

[32] Feb. 28, 1952, *CPD*, House, CCXVI, 598.
[33] See article on Prime Minister Chifley by K. E. Beazley, M. P., *Canberra Times*, March 3, 1966.
[34] Feb. 26, 1947, *CPD*, House, CXC, 166. See also K. H. Bailey, "Dependent Areas of the Pacific: An Australian View," *Foreign Affairs*, XXIV, 494-512.

Though there was this general Labor bias against colonialism and sympathy for the aspirations of dependent territories, the common experiences and cooperation with the Dutch in the war against Japan complicated the matter for the government. This is evident from remarks Evatt made in Parliament in 1944:

Our relations with the Netherlands East Indies are of the most intimate character. We have received great aid from them, and we have, in turn, rendered great aid to them. . . . There is in Australia today the nucleus of the government of the Netherlands East Indies, which will resume occupation of its territory after the war. But we do not talk of these things every day, because the relationship between Australia and the Netherlands East Indies is so close, so friendly and so accepted.[35]

For a man like Evatt this was very sentimental language, and, moreover, it implied Australian support for the return of the Dutch to the East Indies.

Chifley was moderate in his views. When the troubles began in the Netherlands Indies, he expressed the opinion, which he repeated in 1947, that "an arrangement should be worked out between the Dutch and the Indonesian people whereby the Indonesians, while continuing to enjoy the advantage of the administrative ability of the Dutch, should be given an increasing part in the government of their own country. Ultimately, something of that kind must be done. . . . The Australian Government is not taking sides in the dispute, and has never made any attempt to do so."[36]

On the other hand, the Liberal opposition was kinder toward the Indonesians than might have been expected. Percy Spender, who became minister of external affairs when the Liberal and Country coalition came into power in 1949, expressed his admiration for the Dutch colonial administra-

[35] July 19, 1944, *CPD*, House, CLXXIX, 235.
[36] Sept. 25, 1947, *CPD*, House, CXCIII, 242.

tion and said that he favored the closest economic and strategic collaboration with the Dutch people. He continued: "But we have a direct interest in the future development of the Netherlands East Indies. We must remember that the native inhabitants have a civilization 2,000 years old. They have survived invasions of Muhammedans and Hindus and intrusions by the Chinese. As a nation, these people are of vital significance to Australia, and I emphasize the importance of our developing a recognition and understanding of their problems."[37]

Menzies at this time assumed and hoped that the Dutch administration would be restored after the war, but he also recognized "the profound future importance" of the East Indies for Australia, because they represented "not only a military and political barrier reef to Northwest Australia but also in the future trading of the world, they present great possibilities of friendly association and mutual development. I would never exclude them from even the smallest picture of the responsibilities and interests of Australia."[38]

The Indonesian nationalists undoubtedly were aware of where the Australian government's sympathy lay. The Australians, however, until the first "police" action by the Dutch, remained impartial, at least officially, in the conflict between the Netherlands and its dependency.

Ten days after the Dutch resorted to force, the Australian government brought the conflict before the Security Council of the United Nations, which ordered a cessation of hostilities and created a Committee of Good Offices. The Republic of Indonesia designated Australia as its choice to serve on the Committee, while the Netherlands chose Belgium. The governments of Australia and Belgium selected the United States to serve as the third member. From this time until the Netherlands and Indonesia agreed upon terms for Indo-

[37] July 18, 1944, *CPD*, House, CLXXIX, 110.
[38] July 18, 1944, *CPD*, House, CLXXIX, 105.

nesia's independence, the Australian representatives strongly supported Indonesia's position and were sharply critical of the Dutch. When the Dutch resorted to a second police action in December, 1948, Australia strongly condemned the Netherlands and even accused it of bad faith. It suggested that the Netherlands be expelled from the United Nations.[39] The Australian government sent a delegation to the New Delhi conference called by India's Prime Minister Nehru to discuss the Indonesian question and to pressure the Security Council to intervene. At this conference Australia demonstrated its support of the Asian countries on the issue of colonialism. An important factor was the attitude of the Australian trade unions, which shortly after the Indonesian declaration of independence had imposed a ban on Dutch shipping, Dutch air services, and the movement of Dutch goods within Australia, thus supporting the government's policy of preventing the shipment of arms to Indonesia.

The Labor government's policy undoubtedly won Australia considerable Indonesian good will. Later events and problems have put relations between the two countries under a strain, but not all of the good will has been dissipated.[40]

The Liberal opposition was not happy about the Labor government's policy toward Indonesia. While it favored self-government for colonial peoples, it warned against premature independence and the abject abandonment of legitimate material interests. Moreover, retention of these areas by the older colonial countries as long as possible was in Australia's interest. Menzies said, "In plain terms, we have been assisting to put the Dutch out of the East Indies. If

[39] U.N., Security Council, *Official Records*, No. 133, Dec. 23, 1948, p. 11.

[40] On the Australian side the following interesting conclusion is reached by a Labor M.P.: "There is no doubt that the moral credit of Chifley's policy was diminished in the eyes of the Australian electorate by two factors. The first was the boycott of Dutch ships on the Australian water front. Chifley was constantly invited to borrow his foreign policy back from the Communists on the wharves. The second was the brainless, needless cruelties to which the Dutch were subjected in Indonesia." K. E. Beazley in the *Canberra Times*, March 9, 1966.

we continue to do that the same process will no doubt, in due course, eject the British from Malaya and the Australians from Papua and New Guinea."[41] Menzies believed that the dispute essentially fell within the domestic jurisdiction of the Netherlands and pointed out that Australia at San Francisco had supported the inclusion of the domestic jurisdiction clause in the Charter of the United Nations "because, to be perfectly plain, that clause was designed to safeguard Australia's right to maintain the White Australian policy. . . . I am at a complete loss to understand by what process of reasoning Australia should be the first country to abandon it in the case of the Netherlands East Indies . . . a handful of malcontents on the Australian water front having taken sides in the matter the Australian government suddenly abandons the domestic jurisdiction clause. . . . The day will come when we shall regret that we succeeded."[42]

Many Australians were uneasy about Sukarno's leadership, and they found it difficult to forget his collaboration with the Japanese, however this might be explained. Since Australians also were worried about Communism in Indonesia, they found themselves in a dilemma. A western-controlled administration might have advantages for the security of Australia, but a colonial government unwanted by its subject peoples would not constitute an effective barrier against another Asian aggression. The best that Australia could hope for was a stable, strong, friendly, independent Indonesia. To develop and maintain good neighborly relations with Indonesia would not be easy, however, as the Australians soon discovered. Australia was concerned about the attitude which an independent Indonesia would develop toward the "white Australia" policy, for Java has a higher population density than any area of similar size in the world.

[41] Quoted by H. A. Wolfson, "Australian Foreign Policy and the Indonesian Dispute," Paper No. 2, Studies submitted by Australian Institute of External Affairs as preparatory papers for the Eleventh Conference of the Institute of Pacific Relations at Lucknow, 1950.
[42] Sept. 24, 1947, *CPD*, House, CXCIII, 177.

As minister for external affairs, Herbert V. Evatt shaped Australia's foreign policy in the critical, formative years, during the war and early postwar period. He was a highly controversial figure; evaluations of his politics and achievements vary widely. This was apparent in the editorial comments at his death in 1965. The *Sydney Morning Herald* concluded that "for the most part Dr. Evatt's career was a disaster. As minister for external affairs and president of the United Nations Assembly he certainly won Australia much attention but his real achievements were exaggerated by publicity and the public never knew the havoc he created in his own department."[43] An interesting, subtly critical view of Evatt is given by the Australian journalist, Donald Horne. Evatt, he wrote, had little concern "for questions of power of any kind apart from getting representation on United Nations committees." He pushed the rapidly expanded External Affairs Department into "every world problem that could be detected." "This," Horne writes, "was the period when the Labor Party Government saw Australia as one of the consciences of the world, the literate vote of the smaller powers and an opponent of colonialism in South East Asia— where Australia assisted in the destruction of Dutch rule in Indonesia."[44]

While Evatt devoted himself with considerable skill and energy to the solution of foreign policy problems on a global basis, he sometimes was strangely oblivious to the immediate tasks. He spoke much of the need for Australians to under-

[43] Nov. 3, 1965. In this connection it may be noted that Hasluck, a senior member of the External Affairs Ministry, resigned in 1947 on the ground that the minister had debased the department by making it "an acquiescent echo" of his will. "Reluctantly I was forced to the opinion that the present Minister for External Affairs does wish to make the diplomatic staff and the staff of the Department of External Affairs his personal possession." Statement made in a lecture at the University of West Australia, quoted in House of Representatives by Menzies. *CPD*, House, CXCIII, 177-79. About two decades later Hasluck became Minister for External Affairs.

[44] *Foreign Affairs*, XLIV, April, 1966, 448-49.

stand Asian peoples and to develop friendly relations with them, but apparently little, if anything, was done while he presided over the External Affairs Department to establish contact with the Asians. In reply to an attack by Evatt on the Liberal government's foreign policy in which he charged that it had "no positive plan for promoting peace in South East Asia, East Asia, or elsewhere," External Affairs Minister Casey said that "we took over no relations with Asia at all. The last Government had completely ignored Asia. We had no relations of any sort with Asian countries." Australia, he said, had no diplomatic posts and no observers. "No effort of any sort had been made in those fateful and formative years to find out what was going on, or to try to help the people in their travail under the lash of Communism in Southeast Asia. Not one thing."[45]

A sympathetic judgment, and certainly one with an understanding of Evatt's significance for Australian diplomatic history, is that of a Melbourne newspaper:

As they stand, the achievements of the 1945-49 period were substantial. Australia was regarded as a "middle power." Asian communities looked to us for advice. We had a positive view of the future of the Commonwealth. It is probable, as Dr. Evatt claimed, that Australia's representation largely influenced India and Pakistan to stay within the Commonwealth when they gained independence. We took a leading role in bringing the Indonesion peoples' struggle against the Dutch to the Security Council. The good will which this brought in Indonesia has been very greatly reduced in later conflicts but perhaps not entirely lost. Much of the ardor, idealism and hope of the Evatt era has gone.[46]

[45] April 27, 1955, *CPD*, House, VI, 210.
[46] *Melbourne Herald*, Nov. 3, 1965. Friends and foes alike recognized that Evatt left his mark on Australian history. An interesting point of view was that of *The Australian:* "while never absolutely successful at home, he was absolutely necessary for Australia abroad." Nov. 3, 1965.

4 Indonesian "Confrontation"-- West New Guinea

Indonesia, in default of any legal claim, lacking in any justification or any reason apart from self-aggrandizement, threatened to invade West New Guinea unless it was handed over to them. The country was administered by our old friends and staunch allies, the Dutch. Of Indonesia it is unnecessary to say much except that the Sukarno Government is a military dictatorship, subject to Communist influence, that it lives upon blackmail and that its wretched subjects receive little benefit from the aid poured out by the Western world, their condition is worse than in the days of the Dutch, their economic outlook desperate. As to the people of West New Guinea themselves, this is another matter. They are our friends, closely related to our own people of Papua and New Guinea; as yet primitive, but anxious and surely entitled to march to nationhood in their own way. They did not wish to join with Indonesia, and with good reason. Yet Australia raised no voice for this defenseless minority.

H. B. GULLET
Chief Whip for the Liberal-Country Government in Parliament, 1950-1955.
Forces in Australian Politics (Melbourne, 1963), 87.

AUSTRALIA'S MOST IMPORTANT diplomatic problem is the relationship with its nearest neighbor, the newly independent Indonesia. Relations began hopefully enough. In March, 1950, the new Liberal minister for external affairs, Percy Spender, expressed considerable optimism in his statement on foreign policy in the House. He had spent several days in Djakarta and had had an opportunity to meet President Sukarno and most of his cabinet. "I formed the conclusion," he stated, "that they were able men with moderate views and a sober realization of the immensity of the tasks before them. . . . There is, I believe, no question of their distaste for communism and their determination to resist it in whatever form it may take." It would be the government's policy, he said, to foster contacts with the governments of Southeast Asian countries. "We will be helping to provide them and ourselves with the best defence against the effective penetration of communist infiltration."[1]

The development of good relations with Indonesia was not to be an easy matter. The internal political developments in Indonesia, especially after 1955, did not tend to promote friendly relations between the two countries. Moreover, first the dispute between Indonesia and the Netherlands over West New Guinea, followed almost immediately by Indonesia's "confrontation" policy against Malaysia, put Australian-Indonesian relations under severe strain.

When the Netherlands formally granted independence to the Republic of the United States of Indonesia on December 27, 1949, an important issue between the two countries remained unresolved—the status of West New Guinea, or West Irian, as the Indonesians called it. In order not to delay Indonesian independence, the two parties adopted a vague formula which settled nothing and caused more trouble. The

[1] *Commonwealth Parliamentary Debates*, House, CCVI, 628.

status quo of the territory would be maintained with the stipulation that within a year the question of the political status of West New Guinea would be determined by negotiations between the Republic of Indonesia and the Kingdom of the Netherlands.

Australians, Labor and non-Labor alike, were deeply concerned about the future status of West New Guinea. The Round Table Agreement between the Dutch and the Indonesians hardly had been signed before arguments that Australia had a third-party interest in the territory which the government had a responsibility to press were advanced. A few believed that it might be best if the Dutch were out of West New Guinea, for as long as they remained, the territory would be a focal point for trouble. Indonesia would be suspicious of Dutch intentions, fearful that they would use the territory as a base from which to conquer Indonesia.[2]

By making numerous announcements and declarations President Sukarno began at once to mount a relentless drive for the "recovery" of West New Guinea as an integral part of Indonesia. More than that, he appealed for Australia's assistance in settling the issue on the basis that Indonesia's claim was just. He warned that it would be better for Australia to have Indonesia as a friend next door in New Guinea rather than as a suspicious and discontented neighbor.

On June 8, 1950, Spender presented the government's view, saying that "the separate and distinct nature" of West New Guinea was recognized by the Dutch in their administration of Netherlands Indies. This, as well as the affinity of the territory with the rest of New Guinea, also was recognized when the South Pacific Commission was established with the Netherlands as a member on behalf of West New Guinea.

[2] W. M. Bourke, March 23, 1950, *CPD*, House, CCVI, 1158. He suggested that Australia might buy the territory from the Dutch, as if Indonesia would accept that as a solution.

It is our view that should discussions between the Netherlands and Indonesia tend towards any arrangements which would alter the status of West New Guinea, the matter is no longer one merely for those two parties themselves. This is not simply an assertion. Quite apart from Australia's interest, one obvious consideration is the interest and desires of the people who inhabit this area, their ethnic origins, their affinity with the people of the rest of New Guinea, and other related factors.[3]

Evatt, now leader of the opposition, agreed completely with Spender's views. The problem was of "tremendous importance," he declared. Primarily, it was a matter between Indonesia and the Netherlands, which meant that there could be no change in the status of the territory without the consent of the Netherlands, "but I entirely agree that the interest of Australia in such a settlement is not indirect, but very direct. The interest should and can be adequately safeguarded. The sovereignty of the Netherlands in Western New Guinea is undoubted, and if the Netherlands Government wishes to retain that sovereignty, the situation cannot be altered except by acts of aggression on the part of Indonesia."[4] When the South Pacific Commission was established, the question of including West New Guinea was examined carefully. All experts in the field agreed that there is a sharp line dividing New Guinea from Indonesia and the rest of the Malay archipelago, that "all ethnic considerations preclude the attachment of West New Guinea to Indonesia," that it has no relation to Southeast Asia but is "part and parcel of the South Pacific." A change of status of West New Guinea, Evatt concluded, might threaten the security of Australia and the whole region. He suggested a United Nations trusteeship for West New Guinea as a solution, with

[3] *CPD*, House, CCVIII, 3973.
[4] *CPD*, House, CCVIII, 3973. Evatt stated that in case of Indonesian aggression, "of course, United Nations intervention would immediately result."

Australia either as the sole trustee or one of several. Or Australia might purchase the territory if the Dutch wanted to dispose of it.[5]

Several other Labor members expressed the same views. Calwell, then deputy leader of the opposition, to the end of the struggle was emphatic on the question. He referred to the statement made by Muhammad Yamin, the "foreign minister of the ramshackle Indonesian Republic," that Indonesia demanded control not only of West, but of all New Guinea. "I hope that when the Minister of External Affairs makes a statement on this subject . . . he will indicate that we reject out of hand—I use his phraseology—the claim of Indonesia to Australian New Guinea, and also that he will say definitely that Australia will not permit Indonesia to occupy any portion of Dutch New Guinea." He criticized the government for raising the Australian representative at Djakarta to ambassador. Australian foreign policy "should not continue to have as one of its cornerstones friendship with Indonesia and other countries, the leaders of which were noted for their collaboration with the Japanese."[6]

It was obvious that Australian leaders were worried about the effect the transfer of administration of West New Guinea from the Dutch to the Indonesians would have on the peoples of East New Guinea and Papua. Evatt, in his speech, had observed that Australia's duty to advance the interests of the native peoples would be affected by an Indonesian administration of West New Guinea. "An Asiatic race would be coming into direct contact with the natives of New Guinea in all aspects of their life, because there is no substantial difference between the natives of West New Guinea and those of the rest of New Guinea. That would be to the obvious detriment to the peoples of New Guinea." Spender

[5] *CPD*, House, CCVII, 3975-76. There should be no change in the status of Dutch New Guinea "without the full consent of Australia," he declared on March 16, 1950, *ibid.*, 918.
[6] *CPD*, House, CCVIII, 3893-94.

agreed, pointing out that the Charter of the United Nations emphasized the duty of its signatories to advance the interests of native peoples. "I believe," he said, "that the interests of the natives of New Guinea would be most detrimentally affected by the vesting in any Asiatic power of sovereignty over West New Guinea. The tribal life of the natives would gradually disappear."[7]

The debate over West New Guinea, however, did reveal a difference in attitude between the government and the Labor opposition about the method of implementing Australian policy. Evatt said that it was vital that Australia do more than make public statements about West New Guinea and that it should bring the matter before the United Nations.[8] This was a characteristic attitude of the opposition under Evatt's leadership—to take everything to the United Nations. This point of view was criticized sharply by government leaders "as though that were a cure-all for every malady and as though that were a policy sufficient for every crisis." The United Nations, they argued, can do no more than reflect the prevailing standard of conduct among nations. It was not "an oracle moving by its own impulses."[9] But Evatt pointed out that Australia could not get a real voice in the settlement "unless or until we are at a meeting, whether a United Nations or a committee meeting."[10]

IN AUGUST, 1950, SPENDER visited The Hague for the purpose, it would seem, of encouraging the Dutch government to resist the Indonesian claims at the forthcoming conference between the two governments. "It is important," he said in a public statement, "that we should at this stage make our views plain to the world as well as to the two parties at

[7] Speech of June 8, 1950, *CPD*, House, CCVIII, 3973 ff.
[8] Nov. 28, 1950, *CPD*, House, CCXI, 3182.
[9] Paul Hasluck, April 11, 1957, *CPD*, House, XIV, 788-89.
[10] Nov. 28, 1950, *CPD*, House, CCXI, 3182-83.

this conference." His statement was similar to his speech in Parliament. Because the inhabitants of New Guinea were still a primitive society and a different people from the Indonesians, the transfer of sovereignty would only mean that the native peoples of West New Guinea would "come under the rule of another power but not under the rule of their own people." It was hardly consistent with modern ideas that a million people who were not yet politically conscious should be transferred from one country's sovereignty to another's without their will having been ascertained or being ascertainable. He said that "if the claim of Indonesia to Dutch West New Guinea were conceded to any degree at all, it would be but a matter of time, no matter how genuine may be the assurances to the contrary, when the claim will be pushed further so as to include the Trust Territory of Australian New Guinea and its people." Experience had shown that the island was strategically vital to Australia's defense, and since Australians could not alter their geography, this was supremely important to them. He noted the increasing Communist pressure in Asia. Communism had not yet obtained a foothold in Australian New Guinea, and Australia wanted to insure that it would not. "Australia," Spender concluded in his statement, "has no other motives or aspirations than the interests of the people of New Guinea and its own security, which is also theirs."[11]

The Dutch and the Indonesians did not settle the West New Guinea issue within the year stipulated by the annex to The Hague Round Table Agreements. The two governments took positions inconsistent with their previous views and, in effect, switched arguments. Indonesia, which had based its struggle for independence upon the right of all peoples to self-determination, used a purely juridical-historical argument in this case, claiming to be the successor to the old

[11] Department of External Affairs, *Current Notes* (hereafter cited as *Current Notes*), 1950, XXI, 592-93.

Netherlands Indies of which West New Guinea had been an integral part. This constituted a recognition of the legal validity of colonial claims. The Netherlands, which had ignored self-determination and argued that the difficulties in its dependency were wholly a matter of domestic jurisdiction, largely abandoned juridical arguments and now supported the claims of the natives of West New Guinea, as a distinct people separate from the Indonesians, to the right of self-determination. Moreover, the Indonesian government maintained that at The Hague the two governments had agreed to include West New Guinea in independent Indonesia and that all that had been left unsettled was the time and the manner of the transfer. To counter the Dutch and Australian arguments that the Papuans constituted a distinct ethnic group from the Indonesians, Foreign Minister Subandrio argued that the Indonesian national structure was "developed by our forefathers many centuries ago and which resulted in a historical and traditional association of all the various parts of Indonesia. That structure was taken over by the Netherlands and, in fact, further preserved in its traditional entity." Indonesian unity was not based upon a theory of racial or ethnic solidarity.[12]

The governments were so far apart in their interpretation of the agreement that the protracted negotiations were futile. In 1954, Indonesia brought the dispute before the General Assembly of the United Nations, hoping for some intervention by that body. When the matter came before the General Committee, Australia sought and obtained a hearing to oppose inscription of the item on the agenda on the grounds that Indonesia had no case and that a debate on the subject before the world organization would only further embitter

---

[12] U.N., General Assembly, *Official Records*, 12th Sess., Plenary Meetings (1957), 282. As a matter of fact, Dutch administration in West New Guinea dates only from the third decade of this century, and then only along the coast.

relations between Indonesia and the Netherlands. Spender, the Australian representative, later presented the same argument in detail to the First Committee.

Australia and the Netherlands requested that the General Assembly ask the International Court of Justice for an advisory opinion on the issue of sovereignty, but Indonesia insisted that this was a matter for the General Assembly or the Security Council, because, it argued, the refusal of the Netherlands government to transfer administration of the territory to Indonesia constituted a threat to the peace.

President Sukarno warned the world that if Indonesia obtained no satisfaction from the United Nations it would resort to more direct methods of acquiring control over the disputed territory. When Indonesia failed in 1957 to obtain United Nations intervention in the dispute, Foreign Minister Subandrio stated in the General Assembly that "as the Assembly has not succeeded in bringing the parties together, we have no alternative but action outside the United Nations." He went on to address a few sharp words to "our closest neighbor, Australia." "Our security interests are interlocked," he said. "In this context, the Indonesian people do not understand why the Australian government has aspirations toward West Irian. Either in terms of defense or economics, Indonesia as a whole is far more important for Australia than the territory of West Irian alone." Indonesians hope that "the establishment of a close friendship will not be jeopardized by the incomprehensible attitude of the Australian government on the problems of West Irian."[13]

After 1957 both Indonesia and the Netherlands moved in different directions. Indonesia decided upon a policy of "confrontation"—the display of force, and, if necessary, the resort to force to obtain control of the territory. Indonesia received assistance from Russia, the United States, and the

[13] Nov. 29, 1957, U.N., General Assembly, *Official Records*, 12th Sess., Plenary Meetings, 548-49.

United Kingdom in building up its armed forces. In putting down a serious revolt which broke out in Sumatra and other outer islands in the early months of 1958, the Indonesians acquired military experience and gained confidence. Apparently, President Sukarno hoped that the national crusade to force the Dutch to yield on West New Guinea would unify his badly divided country.

The Netherlands reacted by strengthening their defense forces in New Guinea and with a shift in policy. The Dutch relinquished the idea of a continued exclusive control of the territory and emphasized the Papuans' right to self-determination. The political development of the Papuans was accelerated in 1960 by the establishment of a New Guinea Council that was in part appointed and in part elected. Finally, in 1961, the Netherlands government proposed to the United Nations that it supervise the further preparation of the Papuans for self-determination.

IN OCTOBER, 1957, the Indonesian minister of information launched a campaign for the "liberation" of West New Guinea. Not long after, on November 6, 1957, the Australian and Dutch governments issued a joint statement of cooperation in New Guinea, saying that since the territories and peoples for whose administration they were responsible were geographically and ethnically related, cooperation in policy between the administering states would benefit the Papuans. Their policies were based upon the interests and inalienable rights of the inhabitants in conformity with the provisions and the spirit of the United Nations Charter. Hence, they would coordinate their policies in political, economic, social, and educational development of the inhabitants until the Papuans would be ready to determine their own future.

Naturally, the Indonesian government reacted quite strongly to the joint statement, condemning it as an attempt to influence world opinion against Indonesia's claim to West New Guinea and hinting that it might be the first step toward a military alliance between Australia and the Netherlands. There were rumors that Australia had sent troops to Merauke in Dutch New Guinea. The Indonesian foreign minister used the forum of the United Nations to warn Australia and the Netherlands: "If Indonesia were to conclude that such an alliance did in fact exist and threatened its national security, it would have to adjust itself to the exigencies of the new situation."[14] Australia's External Affairs Minister Casey denied this "fantastic story," which he said had its origin in "a deliberate campaign of falsification from the mouths of responsible ministers of the government of Indonesia."[15]

Neither the Indonesian nor the Australian governments could understand the other's position, though both recognized that the security of the two countries was in many ways interlocked. Indonesian leaders seemed to suspect that Australia wished to acquire control over West New Guinea, however, and they regarded this attitude as unreasonable. Whether in terms of defense or economics, friendly relations with Indonesia were far more important for Australia than the territory possibly could be. Australians were baffled by the Indonesians' drive for control of the territory, especially at this time of national trouble. Why would a government risk war to acquire the power to administer a poor, vast, sparsely settled territory with an almost impenetrable interior at a time when it was facing an acute economic crisis and was threatened with regional revolts and political disintegration? The Australian government did not believe that Sukarno was serious in his threat of confrontation, but the Australians, and also, probably, the Dutch government, miscalculated. The internal divisions within Indonesia did

[14] Nov. 20, 1957, U.N., General Assembly, First Committee, 12th Sess. (1957), 200.
[15] Nov., 1957, *Current Notes,* XXVIII, 882.

not deter but rather drove Djakarta into the campaign for "liberation" of West New Guinea, because it proved to be one policy on which all elements in the population and in the power structure could unite.

WHEN THE RESOLUTION calling for resumption of negotiations between Indonesia and the Netherlands was not adopted by the General Assembly, Sukarno launched the confrontation movement against the Dutch. Dutch enterprises in Indonesia were seized, and thousands of Netherlanders left for home. Australia offered to assist in evacuating the Dutch refugees and to receive them as settlers. On December 12, after a cabinet meeting which discussed the Indonesian situation, the minister of external affairs made a statement advising the Indonesian government to consider both "quietly and justly" the ultimate consequences if, as a relatively weak nation, it disregarded the United Nations and if, as a poor nation, it encouraged actions which "will gravely discourage the introduction of foreign capital."[16]

The Indonesian armed forces had no great difficulty in quelling the revolt which had broken out in Sumatra, and they were eager to win new laurels. Sukarno, the army, and the Communist party were anxious to outdo each other in supporting confrontation, and Russia willingly provided the military equipment to threaten and, if necessary, to make war against a colonial power.

The Australian-Netherlands joint statement of policy in New Guinea committed the two powers to promote self-determination for the inhabitants of the island. This emphasis upon the interests and ultimate wishes of the inhabitants was a wise policy, for it lessened, if it did not silence, the charges of colonialism. It cost the Dutch little, and they were becoming weary of the matter and had begun to look for a way

[16] Dec. 1957, *Current Notes,* XXVIII, 978-79.

out without too much loss of face. By clinging to the territory they stood to lose their investments in Indonesia. In addition, the administration of West New Guinea was costing the Netherlands about $30,000,000 a year. Defense costs, even without considering possible war a long distance from home, could drive this amount into staggering sums for a small country like the Netherlands.

The situation for Australia was quite different. New Guinea was practically contiguous to Australia and was important to Australia's security. The inhabitants might choose to become a part of Australia or to remain associated with it in some form, but there was no guarantee of this.[17]

The West New Guinea issue produced several worries for Australia. If the Netherlands decided to withdraw or to make a deal with Indonesia, Australia would be left in an awkward, difficult position. There was also the question of the nature and the importance of the New Guinea issue in Indonesian politics. Did it play into the hands of the Communists? Was Australia faced with the choice of yielding as gracefully as possible to help to keep a non-Communist regime in power, or of keeping West New Guinea from being taken over by Indonesia and in so doing possibly be aiding Communist attempts to acquire control over the government? Another concern was the attitude of the United States, whose attitude had been neutral, and possibly ambiguous. If the United States should decide to support Indonesia, or if it should remain neutral, Australia would find itself in an extremely precarious position.

The Australian government at this stage had broad popular support for its policies. The Labor party in Parliament offered little criticism, but neither did it make helpful suggestions. Evatt referred to Casey as a man of good will

[17] There would also be the remote possiiblity of West New Guinea, as well as both parts of East New Guinea, electing to become Australian, in which case Australia would be the gainer, but such a development would not be acceptable to Indonesia.

who organizes his SEATOS "for the purpose of opposing radical, socialist-democratic or Communist governments" but has no positive proposals in crucial matters.[18] In the interest of friendship with both the Netherlands and Indonesia, Evatt urged the government to seek a summit meeting to negotiate a regional pact providing for cooperation in upholding the security and welfare of New Guinea and Indonesia. Casey believed that such a pact would be no solution to the present problem, which was solely one of disputed sovereignty. Evatt admitted this, but he maintained that without some such step the sovereignty problem could not be settled. Beyond that, Evatt fell back on his familiar charge that the government lacked faith in the United Nations and that it should bring all problems to the world organization.[19]

WITH THE VISIT to Canberra of Subandrio in February, 1959, Australia's position on West New Guinea shifted, though both Casey and Menzies stoutly denied this. The joint communique issued at the conclusion of Subandrio's visit stated that while the difference in the positions of the two governments concerning West New Guinea remained, "the position was clarified by an explanation from the Australian Ministers that it followed from their position of respect for agreements on the rights of sovereignty that if any agreements were reached between the Netherlands and Indonesia as parties principal, arrived at by peaceful processes, and in accordance with internationally accepted principles, Australia would not oppose such an agreement."[20]

The joint announcement caused a furor in Australia, and many were convinced that it indicated a change of policy. Some regarded it as a sellout of the Papuans' right to determine their own destiny. There was widespread fear that the

[18] April 2, 1957, *CPD*, House, XIV, 420-21.
[19] April 2, 9, 11; Dec. 5, 1957, *CPD*, House, XIV, 568-81; 2921-56.
[20] *Current Notes*, XXX, 81.

joint statement presaged giving Indonesia control over West
New Guinea. To prevent this a wide range of suggestions
were made: that Australia place the issue before the United
Nations, that Australia attempt to purchase the territory from
the Netherlands, and that East and West New Guinea be
placed under a joint Australian-Netherlands administration.

For the Labor party, New Guinea presented an especially
difficult problem, and Labor leaders never developed a consistent policy on New Guinea. Their views reflected a mix-
ture of strident nationalism and white Australianism. Evatt,
the parliamentary leader, was sharply critical of the communique. All that it did, he charged, was to say that Australia
would have no objections if Indonesia obtained sovereignty
over West New Guinea from the Netherlands. He did not
think that any question of sovereignty was involved. In the
old, technical, and legal sense sovereignty resided where it
had resided since 1949, with the Netherlands. The vital
question was in whose interest was the territory to be governed? It had to be governed according to the Charter of
the United Nations, which meant that it must be governed
in the interests of the native peoples, but there was no suggestion of this in the joint statement, Evatt said. Moreover,
all New Guinea was vital to the security and defense of
Australia. The government immediately should reconsider
its policy upon a basis of frankness with Indonesia. He
pressed the Labor party's policy of a mutual regional pact
for the security and welfare of the peoples concerned as the
solution to the problem.[21]

Casey explained that the government had merely stated
its attitude toward a hypothetical situation in which Indo-

[21] Feb. 18, 1959, *CPD*, House, XXII, 39. The official statement of the
party's policy to which Evatt referred is found in Decision 14 of the 1955
A.L.P. Conference and reads as follows: "A mutual regional pact for security
and welfare should be negotiated between Australia, Holland and Indonesia.
The pact should aim at promoting the security of the entire areas of
Indonesia and New Guinea. It should also aim at improving the standards
of life for all the peoples throughout the area—so vital to Australia."

nesia and the Netherlands had reached an agreement about the sovereignty of West New Guinea. In these circumstances named in the joint statement, Australia would not oppose such an agreement. "Believing as we do in the fundamental rights to make agreements possessed by the Netherlands government derived from the sovereignty which we are convinced the Netherlands possesses and believing in the rule of law, this position is the only right and proper one for Australia. It represents no new departure in our policy, but I believe it does clarify to Indonesia a position upon which they have held doubts."[22]

Menzies replied to Evatt at considerable length. Subandrio was told that the Australian government recognized Dutch sovereignty over West New Guinea. If Indonesia disputed this, this question (of sovereignty) should be determined by adjudication or agreement. If sovereignty was to be changed, it must be by legal means. The Australian government was not prepared to urge the Dutch government to negotiate, for Indonesia would agree to negotiation only if it resulted in a transfer of sovereignty. Thus, if Australia urged the Dutch to negotiate, it could only be interpreted as an indication of Australia's desire to see a change in the sovereignty over the territory. This would be a reversal of policy, and his government would not do this. Should Indonesia and the Netherlands reach an agreement on the question of sovereignty, Australia would respect it, but it would continue to be concerned about the future of the indigenous population. Australia was preparing the natives of East New Guinea for self-determination and expected similar practices to be followed in West New Guinea. Of great importance to Australia was the public affirmation obtained from Indonesia that it would not use force to gain control of the territory.

---

[22] *CPD*, House, XXII, 36. Casey two days later reiterated the government's view that "The simple fact is that the parties principal in this matter of western New Guinea are the Netherlands and Indonesia. . . . Australia is no more and no less than a very interested third party." *Ibid.*, 216.

Prime Minister Menzies argued that it was the Labor party, and not his government, which had changed its views on the matter. Evatt in a speech in Parliament on October 7, 1949, had declared that "sovereignty of Dutch New Guinea is in the Netherlands. . . . From our point of view, the relationship of Dutch New Guinea with the Indonesian Republic and the future government of the territories concerned are matters primarily for the Dutch and Indonesian Governments. . . ." Menzies further criticized Evatt for stating that the dispute was not suited for adjudication by the International Court of Justice, that there was "nothing to decide." While the court might not have automatic or compulsory jurisdiction in the matter, what was to prevent the two disputants from voluntarily agreeing to accept the jurisdiction of the court? If they did, would the Labor party repudiate the decision of the court?[23]

A few members of Parliament saw more behind the joint statement than the government spokesman would admit. Two were convinced that the government was extremely worried that the Netherlands might make a deal with Indonesia. Tremendous pressure was being put upon the political parties and the government of Holland to trade with Indonesia on the basis of the return of the seized properties belonging to Dutch nationals and Dutch corporations in exchange for the transfer of the sovereignty and administration of West New Guinea to Indonesia.[24] One member pointed out the dilemma with which the Australian government was struggling: "Which was the greatest threat, Dutch West New Guinea in hostile hands or a hostile Indonesia?"[25] Casey throughout his period as minister for external affairs had been concerned about Australia's image

[23] *CPD*, House, XXII, 194-95.
[24] B. Donald White and D. H. Drummond, *CPD*, House, XXII, 80 and 118, respectively.
[25] G. W. Anderson, *CPD*, House, XXII, 148.

among Asian peoples. In his opening statement in the debate on the joint communique he noted that while he had visited Indonesia several times, it had been more than seven years since the foreign minister of Indonesia had visited Australia. Contacts such as the visit of the Indonesian foreign minister offered were a way of indicating the "real and sympathetic interest" that Australia has for Indonesia's progress.²⁶ Menzies emphasized that his government did not want the differences over West New Guinea to hurt "the development of sensible friendship and mutual understanding" between the two countries.²⁷ The Australian government also was concerned about the seizure of Dutch properties in Indonesia and about the radical trend of the Indonesian government and the possibility that it might turn to Communist countries for large-scale aid.

It would seem likely that Subandrio was maneuvering to isolate the Netherlands diplomatically and to soften Australia's attitude on the West New Guinea issue. Whether or not the Australian government meant to make some concession to Indonesia, the joint statement did indicate some change of position. Previously, Australia had said that under no circumstances would it tolerate the transfer of West New Guinea to Indonesia's control; it seemed now to have encouraged Indonesia to put pressure on the Netherlands for such a settlement. If Australian leaders intended a new approach to the West New Guinea problem, the public reaction to the joint statement hastily discouraged this. Menzies visited The Hague in July, and after consultation with the new, more conservative Dutch government, he reaffirmed that there had been no change in the policies of the two governments. In December, Menzies visited Djakarta. The atmosphere at the time was favorable for

²⁶ *CPD*, House, XXII, 36.
²⁷ *CPD*, House, XXII, 195.

the Australian leader, because Indonesia was involved in a bitter controversy with Peking concerning the hostile treatment given to Chinese merchants in Indonesia, and frequent references were made to "a common enemy from the North." President Sukarno gave Menzies absolute assurances that he would not resort to force to win control of West New Guinea. The two leaders reaffirmed support of the joint communique of February, and Menzies emphasized self-determination for the Papuans.[28]

RELATIONS BETWEEN AUSTRALIA and Indonesia were relatively calm at the beginning of 1960, but there were indications that the New Guinea issue would soon come to a head. Dutch public opinion was undergoing a rapid shift, as the Dutch had almost adjusted themselves to the loss of their empire and were becoming more European in their outlook. The country was enjoying great prosperity, which was largely ascribed to the movement for European economic integration in which the Netherlands had played a leading role. The Common Market could do as much, and probably more, for the expansion of Dutch industrial activity than could their lost empire. In any case, their empire, except for a poor and costly remnant, was gone, and for a small country like Holland the Common Market opened new vistas. Moreover, the illusions about New Guinea were disappearing rapidly as it became clear that the vast territory had few natural resources, and that the administration of the distant dependency was a drain on the Netherlands treasury.[29] The territory offered only psychological compensation, and this was diminishing rapidly. Just as it became

---

[28] See the account of the visit by Bruce Grant, an Australian journalist, *Indonesia* (Melbourne, 1964), 159.

[29] The direct annual subsidy increased from 68,500,000 guilders in 1957 to 81,000,000 guilders (about $22,000,000) in 1961.

evident that Indonesia was moving toward the use of military force to achieve its goal in West New Guinea, the Congo tragedy burst. The Dutch had envied Belgium, their next-door neighbor, in its possession of this important tropical colony; they now became frightened at the prospect that West New Guinea might develop into another Congo. The Dutch by 1960 had become anxiously determined to get rid of the dangerous burden of West New Guinea,[30] since a war with a well-armed state on the other side of the world would be a major national disaster.

The Dutch still were determined not to turn the territory over to Indonesia, however. This accounts in part for the accelerated preparation for self-government. They thought that by a crash program of political development they could achieve three objects: (1) discharge their moral obligation to the Papuans on the right of self-determination; (2) prevent Indonesia from acquiring control of the territory; and (3) get rid of the whole troublesome, dangerous problem. However, events moved so rapidly that they did not achieve these goals, and they had become so anxious about the situation that they were willing to accept a compromise settlement. Before doing this, the Netherlands made a last, vain attempt to achieve its goals by offering to transfer the administration of the territory to the United Nations.[31]

An important factor in the decision of the Dutch government to disengage itself from the West New Guinea question was its increasing diplomatic isolation. When the situation became acute, the Netherlands received no support from its friends; instead, it was subjected to severe pressure to yield to Indonesian demands. United States President

[30] For an excellent analysis of the change of Dutch opinion on the West New Guinea issue see Arend Lijphart, *The Trauma of Decolonization: The Dutch and West New Guinea* (New Haven, 1966).
[31] Oct. 3, 1961.

John F. Kennedy, was much concerned about developments in Indonesia and took a personal interest in seeing the dispute settled. According to historian Arthur Schlesinger, the president regarded Indonesia as one of the "potentially significant" countries of Asia. "He was anxious to slow up its drift toward the communist bloc; he knew that Sukarno was already turning to Moscow to get the military equipment necessary for invasion, and he was anxious to strengthen the anti-Communist forces, especially the army, in order to make sure that, if anything happened to Sukarno, the powerful Indonesian Communist Party would not inherit the country." Also he was anxious to avoid a great power confrontation in this remote corner of the world. Kennedy offered Sukarno help in finding a solution to the problem by direct negotiation, and he asked British Prime Minister Harold Macmillan to use his influence to persuade Indonesia and Australia to settle their disputes.[32]

There was no support for the Dutch from any quarter. The Australian government could not afford to make any moves, or even public gestures, to oppose the policy of the United States, supported by Great Britain, and thus it remained discreetly silent. Neither Australia nor the Netherlands, nor both, could afford a war against Indonesia without great-power support. Furthermore, some Australians were beginning to doubt the strategic importance of New Guinea in any future war. An attempt by Prime Minister of Malaya Tengku Abdul Rahman in October, 1960, to mediate a solution to the dispute seems to have had at least the tacit approval of the Australian government, judging from a statement Menzies made to Parliament. Rahman, he said, had consulted him about putting forth proposals, and he in turn conveyed his government's views. Australia believed that the future of the territory should be determined by the

[32] Arthur N. Schlesinger, Jr., *A Thousand Days: John F. Kennedy in the White House* (Boston, 1965), 533-34.

freely expressed will of the inhabitants and that any decisions that might be made between Indonesia and the Netherlands should not be influenced by fear of threats.[33] At first Rahman seemed to make some progress, as after discussions at The Hague with Prime Minister De Quay a joint communique was issued stating that the Netherlands government was willing to subject its policies in West New Guinea to the "scrutiny and judgment" of the United Nations. The tengku's "sacred mission" was wrecked by Indonesia's bitter attacks upon it. Arthur Calwell, who had succeeded Evatt as leader of the Labor opposition, used the discussion of the West New Guinea situation to revive his party's idea of a tripartite agreement.[34]

Shortly after the announcement of its program for the rapid development of self-determination in West New Guinea, the Dutch government strengthened the defenses of the territory by sending out the aircraft carrier, *Karel Doorman*. Indonesian infiltrations had been reported by the Dutch before they began to reinforce their armed forces in the territory, but the Indonesian government called this action provocative and used it to justify an arms buildup in eastern Indonesia. Subandrio spoke of the possibility of an armed clash with the Netherlands. The Dutch apprehended small, armed Indonesian groups which had been landed on the coast of West New Guinea, and their navy intercepted an Indonesian vessel attempting to supply infiltrators. The Dutch government became very anxious about the situation.

Apparently, Djakarta was concerned about Australia's actual, or possible, role in the dilemma created by confrontation. In April, 1961, Indonesia sent General Abdul Haris Nasution, chief of the general staff, to Australia, ostensibly "to promote and strengthen the friendly relations between our countries" and "to clarify the latest political, military,

[33] Dec. 6, 1960, *CPD*, House, XXIX, 3571.
[34] *CPD*, House, XXIX, 3580.

and economic developments in Indonesia, specifically about the West Irian issue."[35] What the purpose of Nasution's visit was can be deduced from Prime Minister Menzies' full statement to Parliament on the mission.[36] He said that he had explained to General Nasution that Australia's interest in New Guinea as an island derived from its desire for the enjoyment by the inhabitants of economic and social progress and a natural interest in the character of its political future. Australia's interest had been formed by the significance of New Guinea in two wars; it did not stem from hostility toward Indonesia. In the dispute between Indonesia and the Netherlands, Australia was only a naturally interested neighbor. The chief point of difference between the two governments on West New Guinea was that Australia recognized Dutch sovereignty over the territory while Indonesia based her claim upon political and historical grounds as part of the old Netherlands Indies. Australia would not withdraw its recognition of Dutch sovereignty, but if the case should be submitted to the International Court of Justice and decided in favor of Indonesia, the Australian government would respect the judgment. Prime Minister Menzies further told General Nasution what his government was doing in East New Guinea in improving living standards, education, and health to a level sufficient to allow the inhabitants to determine their own future. The Dutch were applying similar policies with the same objective.

All of this scarcely satisfied the Indonesian emissary. If this was the position of Australia then it should be strictly neutral in the dispute and the discussions between Indonesia and Holland and should not encourage and support the Dutch generally or in the United Nations. That, "he made clear, was the great thing that he wanted to establish with us." At this point Menzies reiterated the three points he

[35] *Sydney Morning Herald*, April 19, 1961.
[36] April 27, 1961, *CPD*, House, XXXI, 1247-48.

pressed upon Subandrio as principles which should be observed in settling the dispute.[37] According to Menzies, Nasution then asked bluntly if there were not some military arrangement with the Netherlands about West New Guinea. Menzies assured him that there were no such arrangements, "directly or indirectly," and he warned Nasution that Australia and other countries would be deeply disturbed by any use of force.[38]

The purpose behind the Nasution mission was quite obvious. Indonesian leaders were convinced that Australia wanted to keep West New Guinea from going to Indonesia and that Australian political support was encouraging the Dutch to resist a settlement with Indonesia. Apparently, they believed that Australia and the Netherlands were working toward a Melanesian federation embracing all New Guinea and the neighboring islands as a means of blocking Indonesian attempts to secure West New Guinea.[39] Djakarta could not hope for Australia's support in the dispute with

[37] See above, p. 53.

[38] In reply to an inquiry by Menzies about the reported infiltrations along the West New Guinea coast, Nasution admitted that there had been some, even armed ones, but said that such cases were not caused by any policy of the central government, but arose from unavoidable lack of control in certain areas. He said that there had also been some infiltrations in reverse.

[39] This belief had some basis. The Australian-Netherlands statement of 1957 was one of several indications in that direction. Dutch Secretary of State for West New Guinea Affairs, Th. H. Bot, on a visit to Canberra in early 1960, proposed that the Netherlands and Australia should work toward political union of the three parts of the island. Some of the Australian ministers were at first receptive to the proposal, but the cabinet rejected it. The ministers of external affairs and of territories were opposed to it. See Gavin Souter, *New Guinea: The Last Unknown* (New York, 1966), 225. Furthermore, the Dutch foreign minister made some pointed comments in March, 1961, stating that a federation of Dutch and Australian New Guinea was "certainly a possibility" and would not lack logic. Both parts of the island were inhabited by the same people and were being led along the same path. The island was divided artificially into two parts; the future of the western part of the island would influence the eastern part. *Sydney Morning Herald*, March 15, 1961. The Netherlands government invited the members of the South Pacific Commission to send representatives to attend the opening of the New Guinea Council (an embryo parliament) in April, 1961. The United States rejected the invitation.

the Netherlands, but it wanted the withdrawal of Australia's support of the Netherlands. If Australia could be induced to take a neutral position, like that of the United States, the Netherlands would yield, so the Indonesians believed. Nasution also was concerned about what Australia would do in case Indonesia occupied West New Guinea or some of the offshore islands, and he wished to reassure Australia that such occupancy would constitute no threat to the security of East New Guinea or Australia. Nasution, as had Subandrio before him, argued persuasively that with the removal of the West New Guinea issue, Australia and Indonesia would inevitably become friends. When Australians countered that this would mean their abandoning of the Dutch, Indonesians replied that perhaps the time had come for Australia to decide which friendship was more important.

Quite naturally, the Australians were aroused when J. M. A. H. Luns, foreign minister of the Netherlands, at the General Assembly meeting in September, 1961, proposed the transfer of the administration of West New Guinea to the United Nations. When asked about it in Parliament, Menzies called the request "a very constructive proposal," but he held little hope that Indonesia would accept it, as it consistently had rejected the principle of self-determination for West New Guinea. Indonesia argued that the territory was part of its domain and that outsiders had no more right to ask for self-determination for West New Guinea than to ask it for Java or Sumatra.[40] Menzies informed the House that the Australian representative addressed the General Assembly on September 27 about Australia's attachment to the principle of self-determination.

IN DECEMBER, 1961, SUKARNO, no doubt encouraged by India's successful seizure of Goa, ordered a general mobili-

[40] Sept. 28, 1961, *CPD*, House, XXXIII, 1444.

zation and threatened to invade West New Guinea. Just as the situation was reaching a crisis point, Australia faced a general election. In the election campaign the Labor party, strongly supported by the *Sydney Morning Herald,* pressed "appeasement of a dictator" as the chief issue. The Liberal-Country coalition won the election, which was held in December, but by a slender, much reduced majority. The election results reflected the strongly hostile reaction of the public to Indonesian bluster, threats, and violence.[41]

Netherlands Prime Minister De Quay on January 2, 1962, announced that his government was ready to resume negotiations on the West New Guinea issue without preliminary conditions. This made the situation so critical that Canberra faced the necessity of making a statement on its policy relating to the negotiations. Two days later the Australian minister for external affairs, Sir Garfield Barwick, in response to an appeal by Subandrio for an understanding of Indonesia's position, issued a statement. It can hardly be called a clarification of the Australian position in the situation, for it was quite noncommittal and was issued in the third person.

The Australian Government's commendation of peaceful and patient negotiation to harmonize the respective views of Indonesia and the Netherlands sprang, not from any misunderstanding of the Indonesian position, but from an understanding both of the Indonesian and the Netherlands points of view. As long ago as the occasion of Dr. Subandrio's visit to Australia, the Australian Government had told the Indonesian Government that it would respect an agreement in accordance with the principles of the United Nations Charter made by Indonesia with the Netherlands in their dispute over West New Guinea provided that agreement was arrived at freely, not under duress or the threat of force. Sir Garfield said that Australia had demonstrated in many ways its desire to promote and maintain the friendliest relations with the people of Indonesia and the Government did

41 See Grant, *Indonesia,* 161-62.

not underestimate the value of Indonesian friendship or of the continuance of peaceful relations between Indonesia and the Netherlands.[42]

Though the Netherlands had practically capitulated, Sukarno was not yet ready to negotiate. He insisted that there be "prior guarantees of success," and to help the Dutch make up their minds he appointed Brigadier Suharto as leader of the Liberation Army. The point had been reached where the Australian government had to make a more definite statement. On January 12, Menzies in effect announced that Australia would follow the lead of the United States in the situation, saying:

This is not a time for either bellicose or extravagant comments. The Government of Australia simply says that it recognizes and will discharge its prime responsibility for the security of Australia, its territories and its people. Having regard not only to our treaty rights and responsibilities but also to the hard facts of international life, we act in close collaboration with the great free Powers, particularly Great Britain and the United States of America. No responsible Australian would wish to see any action affecting the safety of Australia on the issues of war and peace in this area except in concert with our great and powerful friends.[43]

CALWELL ALL ALONG had taken a hard line on the New Guinea issue. In January he strongly criticized Sukarno's speeches, saying that they were reminiscent of Hitler's performances and he accused the government of adopting a

[42] Quoted by Souter, *The Last Unknown*, 227.
[43] Souter, *The Last Unknown*, 228. Obviously to allay Australian apprehensions, Sukarno on January 11 said to an Australian journalist, "We have no ambition for other territories. We just want to free part of our fatherland which is being occupied by Dutch fighting forces." *The New York Times*, Jan. 12, 1962. When Menzies visited Djakarta in December, 1959, Sukarno had assured him that force would not be used to get control of West New Guinea.

"Munich line." The last sentence of the prime minister's statement undoubtedly was a challenge to Calwell to reveal what he and the Labor party would do, and, specifically, whether he would take action contrary to the policy of the United States and Great Britain or in defiance of the two great powers. The prime minister may have deliberately baited a trap for the leader of the opposition. On February 9, Calwell made a lengthy, scathing statement but avoided the trap. Indonesia was threatening to seize New Guinea by force, he said, and the Menzies government proposed to do "precisely nothing" about it. This was "shameful." He called the Indonesian threat "naked imperialism and ruthless colonialism." In this crisis the Labor party supported the United Nations and its Charter, which condemns aggression and calls for the development of friendly relations among nations based upon respect for the principle of equal rights and self-determination of peoples. "Therefore in this crisis we must oppose Indonesian actions which are flagrantly in breach of the United Nations Charter. Further, if Indonesia seeks to deny the principles of the United Nations Charter and to use force to create a potential threat to Australia's security, then, I say, with due regard to the gravity of the situation, that the threat must be faced."[44]

Should Australia take action, regardless of the position of "our great and powerful friends?" Here Calwell seemed rather naive. The government's policy, he said, could be understood only on the basis of three assumptions: "(1) that Australia was so hopelessly ill-prepared that it could make no effective answer to Indonesian aggression, (2) that Indonesian aggression would be condoned by what Mr. Menzies calls 'our great and powerful friends' and that Australia would then be a voice crying in the wilderness against it, (3) that any show of opposition to Indonesia, even by the Dutch, would immediately bring powerful forces from Com-

[44] *Sydney Morning Herald*, Feb. 10, 1962.

munist nations to Indonesia's aid." There was no reason why Australia should stand alone in its opposition to aggression in West New Guinea, "for it had friends who shared its principles and ideals, even if at this moment they did not understand all that was involved." The reason they did not understand was that the Menzies government had done nothing to tell the United States that "an aggressor has begun to undermine the bastion of democracy in the Pacific."[45]

By laying the entire responsibility for the policy of the United States and Great Britain on the Menzies government, Calwell avoided the trap. If Canberra had adequately and forcefully informed Washington and London what was at stake, these countries' policy would have been different. This was no great compliment to the intelligence of the American and British foreign ministers and their departments, but it saved Calwell the necessity of attacking them. However, the disturbing question still remained: what if easing the Dutch out of West New Guinea was the considered policy of Australia's powerful friends and no amount of persuasion from "down under" could cause them to change it?

The prime minister's reply to Calwell was as direct as was diplomatically expedient. If Calwell's statement meant that Australia should be prepared to protect its own territory, including East New Guinea, "the answer is that I said so in plain terms in my statement." If his statement meant that "an Australian Government should convey in relevant quarters its views in favor of self-determination the answer is that our Government has done so on very many occasions, by personal contact and diplomatic channels." If Calwell's statement meant that "without regard to what might be the attitude or action of the Great Powers, Australia should in the event of armed Indonesian aggression against Dutch

[45] *Sydney Morning Herald*, Feb. 10, 1962.

New Guinea, declare war against Indonesia, it is clearly crazy and irresponsible."[46]

In his reply Menzies observed plaintively that it was "an inescapable fact that though we have throughout recognized Dutch sovereignty in West New Guinea, every nation in Asia supported the Indonesian claim." He did not despair of a peaceful and just solution, but the opposition leader's vaguely belligerent views did nothing but harm. He appeared determined "to create an atmosphere which would make it difficult in the future to live in a state of harmony with our neighbors," Menzies said.

The statements clearly indicated a change of policy. The government was in a dilemma. It faced the hard choice of either adhering to its policy of continued diplomatic support of the Netherlands and resistance to Indonesian ambitions to secure West New Guinea without the support and against the policy of its "powerful friends," or of abandoning support of the Dutch and taking a neutral stand on the issue but retaining the good will of the states it depended upon for security. Laborites urged the government to initiate action in the United Nations to compel Indonesia to observe the Charter principles of nonaggression and the right of self-determination, but, as Barwick pointed out, this expedient promised little. The complexion of the United Nations had changed. "In the presence of strong anti-colonial attitudes and the desire to maintain the territorial integrity of newly independent nations, the principle of self-determination is apt to receive less emphasis and indeed to be regarded competitive with, and certainly not paramount to, what are considered to be necessities and urgencies of anti-colonialism."[47] Furthermore, he was certain the measure would bring a Soviet veto in the Security Council.

The government was urged to make commitments about

[46] *Sydney Morning Herald*, Feb. 12, 1962.
[47] March 15, 1962, *CPD*, House, XXXIV, 907.

what it would do in the event of hostilities. Barwick replied that no responsible government would do that when the secretary-general of the United Nations was attempting a negotiated settlement and, furthermore, the facts of international life and Australia's responsibility to the world community made it necessary for the government "to take full account of the attitude of our great allies and of the United Nations."[48]

During this debate Calwell made another of his hard-line speeches. Behind the fine statements of principle of the government spokesmen there lay, he said, "this sickness of defeatism, this readiness to take direction from the people they refer to as our 'great and powerful friends.'" No prime minister or minister for external affairs in the history of the Commonwealth had met the "rebuffs," "humiliations," and "failures" which the present ministers have suffered.[49]

UNDER THE AEGIS of the United Nations and the pressure of the United States, negotiations between the Netherlands and Indonesia proceeded intermittently for several months. A retired American diplomat served as mediator. In the agreement, signed on August 15, 1962, that provided for the transfer of the administration of West New Guinea to Indonesia by May, 1963, the Dutch made an almost complete surrender. They were spared from turning the territory directly over to the Indonesians by an interim administration by the United Nations of a few months' duration. The agreement said nothing about sovereignty, no doubt to spare the feelings of the Dutch, but it left no doubt about the transfer. The right of self-determination that the Dutch had insisted upon so stoutly was embodied in the agreement but in a way that gave it doubtful meaning. The inhabitants are

[48] *CPD*, House, XXXIV, 907.
[49] March 29, 1962, *CPD*, House, XXXIV, 1152ff.

to exercise the right of self-determination by a plebiscite before the end of 1969, after some six years of Indonesian administration.[50] The Netherlands transferred the administration to the United Nations Temporary Executive Authority on October 1, 1962, which turned it over to Indonesia on May 1, 1963. With this agreement for the Dutch the issue came to an end, but it can scarcely be called peaceful settlement. Throughout the final months of negotiation the Dutch were subjected to mounting pressure. Prime Minister De Quay in a radio broadcast told his people that Holland "could not count on the support of its allies, and for that reason we had to sign."[51] The attitude of the United States and Great Britain immobilized Australia, without whose support Dutch resistance was futile. With all possible aid to the Dutch sealed off, Sukarno felt safe in applying increased military pressure on the Dutch in West New Guinea, including armed landings. Unfortunately, the "negotiated" settlement took place under the auspices of the United Nations, whose first purpose is the prevention of threats to the peace, suppression of acts of aggression, and the settlement of international disputes by "peaceful means and in conformity with the principles of justice and international law." However much their pride may have been hurt, the agreement was fortunate for the Dutch, relieving them of a financial burden of about $30,000,000 a year and removing the danger of involvement in a disastrous war.

[50] It may be that Sukarno never intended that such a referendum be held. On April 18, 1965, at the tenth anniversary of the Bandung Conference, he declared, "Why should we have a plebiscite? In the first place West Irian is recognized by the whole world as territory of the Republic of Indonesia; in the second place we are not a member any more of the United Nations." *News and Views*, Consulate General of the Republic of Indonesia, New York. Foreign Minister Adam Malik promised a plebiscite on the future of West Irian would be held. *The New York Times*, Oct. 1, 1966. Two months later, Djakarta announced that, in line with the wishes of the West Irianese people, no plebiscite would be held. *Ibid.*, Dec. 8, 1966.
[51] *The New York Times*, Aug. 17, 1962.

Likely, Washington followed the policy it did because it feared development of a second front in Southeast Asia. Russia supported Indonesia in its confrontation policy by supplying it with armaments worth about a billion dollars. Intensified confrontation certainly would have brought Indonesia into closer association with the Soviet Union. Another important consideration was the relationship between the Indonesian internal politics and West New Guinea. If Sukarno failed to achieve the "recovery" of West New Guinea, would he be pushed aside by greater extremists? Would it enable the Communists to take over? On the other hand, America's tolerance of Sukarno helped him to stay in power and to continue his "revolutionary" policies that, by gutting the economy and delaying reconstruction, provided conditions that aided the Communist party's growth.

As it turned out, the settlement of the West New Guinea dispute freed Indonesia to turn on Malaya, threatening a second front.[52] The result of the armaments buildup of the West New Guinea confrontation was the increased strength of the army that enabled it, in the critical days of the attempted coup and countercoup in the fall of 1965, to suppress the Communist party and to subordinate Sukarno.[53]

ABOUT A WEEK after the agreement was reached, Barwick reported to Parliament on the diplomatic activities of the Australian government in the last months of the dispute.[54] He emphasized that while Australia had no rights or claims to the territory, it had a "real and abiding interest" in a

[52] Sukarno was probably driven to the second confrontation by the instability of the balance of power between the army and the Communist party, which enabled him to remain in power.

[53] If this interpretation of these events is valid, the results for Russia were both a loss and a gain. Communist influence was reduced drastically, but the friendship between Djakarta and Peking was ended abruptly. For Communist China the developments represented sheer loss.

[54] Aug. 21, 1962, *CPD*, House, XXXVI, 512ff.

peaceful settlement of the dispute and in the right of the inhabitants ultimately to choose their own future. Accordingly, the government had maintained "a constant and vigorous diplomatic encouragement" to the disputants to settle their differences peacefully, for warfare would have lessened the chance of the indigenous people to acquire self-determination. He had, therefore, gone to Djakarta twice[55] to convey to the Indonesian leaders the views of his government on the continued use of force, to urge them to return to the conference table and to reach a settlement in which self-determination by the Papuans would be recognized.

Barwick stated further that Australia had never made any military commitment to the Netherlands relating to West New Guinea; the agreements between the Australian and Dutch governments were limited to jointly-agreed-upon principles in administering their respective territories in New Guinea. The Australian government had not "at any time brought any pressure of any kind to bear upon the Netherlands to adopt any particular solution." Barwick concluded that the result of the agreement was "a part of history with which Australia must live . . . if any should have contemplated a military adventure, it is worth remembering that none of the countries of the West, and particularly of those with whom Australia has the closest association, were at any relevant time willing to maintain a Netherlands administration by military means."

For Australians the West New Guinea affair was a bitter, frustrating experience.[56] Indonesia is their most important

[55] At the end of May and again four weeks later.

[56] When Hasluck took over the External Affairs Department from Barwick he is reported as having said: "But sometimes on a big issue—Indonesian conduct in West New Guinea—I found, from what the newspapers said, from what people said or wrote to me, from the report of Parliamentarians, and so on, that Australia as a whole was deeply stirred. People felt that something pretty wrong was being done by Indonesia and they would have liked Australia—and the United States, too—to have taken a much stronger line. That was something which welled up from deep down in the common sense of the Australian people." *The Age*, June 13, 1964.

foreign policy problem, since they know that they must develop friendly relations with their nearest neighbor of 100,000,000 people. They feared that Indonesian occupation of West New Guinea, however, would almost certainly constitute a grave threat to their national security, especially if the Communists should gain control in Djakarta. They felt that the risk was so great that their government should do everything possible to keep Indonesia out of New Guinea. The national view was stated tersely by Sir Percy Spender: "New Guinea will forever be a potential springboard to Australia."[57] The Japanese had taught that "bitter lesson" by their invasion of the island in World War II.

The government's policy was criticized sharply. The influential *Sydney Morning Herald* expressed the sentiments of many Australians when it said in answer to the question of what the Menzies government would do if Indonesia used arms to enforce their claims to West New Guinea: "The answer is that, unless the Government can be driven from the position of weak-kneed acceptance—amounting, at worst to appeasement and at its futile best, to a gentle castigation of Indonesia for breaches of faith—Australia will stand gutless on the side lines. Yet every consideration of national security demands a totally different attitude towards the intrusion into New Guinea of a potential enemy."[58]

[57] Before the First Committee of the General Assembly of the United Nations on Nov. 24, 1954, Casey also emphasized the importance of New Guinea for Australian defense. "Its importance has been clearly demonstrated in two world wars, especially when the Japanese gravely threatened Australia by their landings in New Guinea. It is on our doorstep, and we cannot be indifferent to what becomes of it." *Friends and Neighbors: Australia and the World* (Melbourne, 1954), 102.

[58] Editorial, Feb. 10, 1962. After Menzies' statement of Feb. 10, this journal again expressed its condemnation of the government's policy in scathing terms. Menzies had excused his attitude by pointing out that "every nation in Asia supports the Indonesian claim." "This," said the editorial, "is not only the language of appeasement; it is also the language of pusillanimity. Is Australia to let her national interests to be decided by the Great Power? Is she to stay her hand for fear of offending the nations of Asia?

"There will be few Australians who will read their Prime Minister's state-

The situation proved as difficult for the Labor opposition as it was for the government, and the Labor party revealed a basic inconsistency in its stand. When in power it helped to usher the Dutch out of Indonesia; now that it was in the opposition, it was determined to keep them in the remnant of territory that still belonged to them. Evatt expressed this feeling of frustration at the time of Subandrio's visit to Canberra in 1959. He was opposed to letting the future of the native peoples of New Guinea be "determined by the consent of Holland to the wishes of Indonesia," but he claimed he was "without any feeling against the Indonesians at all." The Labor government had done its "utmost" to help them put their case for self-government before the United Nations. "I would expect," he said, "as a matter of simple gratitude, that Indonesia should recognize what Australia did to help it towards self-government. Now Indonesia is moving into an area peculiarly linked with Australian fortunes, not only in connection with defence, as was very apparent in the great struggle of World War II for New Guinea, but also in relation to our paramount duty to support native development and the ultimate achievement of native self-government in that country. One would think they would stand up and say, 'We think the Australian Government is best fitted to do this; let it do it.' "[59]

___

ment of policy without feelings of shame and foreboding. . . . Here is the undisguised sacrifice of national honor on the altar of expediency. Here, too, is the dangerous and familiar failure to recognize that appeasement feeds aggression and that aggression knows no bounds." Feb. 12, 1962.

[59] Aug. 13, 1959, *CPD*, House, XXIV, 194. He had similarly expressed himself on February 24 in Parliament: "I say that the paramount interest here, now and ultimately is that of the native people. . . . We on this side, will do our best to be on friendly terms with Indonesia. We want to have friendship with that country, but we have a duty, also, to see, primarily that the interests of the native peoples are protected, not in the sweet bye and bye but here and now. We have also to watch Australia's defence. I do not care a fig for those people who say that the question of Australian defence is not inseparably bound up with New Guinea, whatever particular changes in weapons take place. That fact is obvious, and is supported by great military authorities." *Current Notes*, XXX, 90-92.

The Australian government seemed to be guided by four principles: (1) the recognition of Dutch sovereignty, (2) Australian national security, (3) the right of self-determination of the indigenous population, and (4) peaceful settlement. These principles were not wholly consistent. At first the Australian government pressed Netherlands' sovereignty, but with the implication that the Dutch government could not transfer its legal title to the territory without the approval of Australia, because this might endanger Australia's security. Self-determination and peaceful settlement were pressed later, when it became obvious that the first two principles found little support in the world forum and the Dutch began to show signs of weariness and a desire to get rid of the onerous problem, if it could be done without national humiliation. To urge peaceful settlement on the parties had little meaning if it did not include the right to agree to transfer sovereignty over the territory to Indonesia, or to acknowledge that it already resided there. Nor did the argument that the right of self-determination was guaranteed by the Charter of the United Nations to non-self-governing peoples prove very effective in the anticolonial atmosphere which prevailed so widely after World War II. Self-determination was regarded by some as a device to deprive a newly independent country of part of its fatherland.

The Australian government was in an uncomfortable position. Most Australians were convinced that Indonesian sovereignty and administration of West New Guinea would endanger their national security, and this fear increased with the growing influence of the Communist party in Indonesia. Support of the Netherlands exposed it to linkage with colonialism, especially among Asian peoples with whom Australia wished to develop friendly relations. Furthermore, when the "great and powerful friends" on which Australia ultimately relied for national security decided not to support the Netherlands, the Australian government had no alternative but to shift its policy.

The halfhearted gesture of solidarity with the Netherlands by the agreement in 1957 on the policies which the two governments would follow in their respective territories in New Guinea was too weak to cause any modification of Indonesian policy or to win supporters among other states, and it made Australia's problems in the administration of East New Guinea more difficult. The Dutch and Australian policies began to diverge. The former wanted to get out of New Guinea as quickly as possible, while the Australians were in no haste to get out and may not have wished to get out at all. The Australian government did not wish to join the Dutch in their race toward self-determination, and it thought the policy of accelerating the timetable was unwise and dangerous. An economically weak and defenseless state of West New Guinea in the face of a hostile Indonesia could only be a source of trouble. Moreover, the Dutch crash policy of inspiring nationalism in New Guinea was certain to cause repercussions in Australian New Guinea. Lastly, it may be asked whether Australian support did not encourage the Dutch to prolonged, futile resistance and useless sacrifices.

5 Indonesian "Confrontation"-- Malaysia

The people of this country should be clear in their own minds about Australia's stake in the region it shares with Indonesia. A weak, unstable and economically struggling Indonesia must affect the strength, stability and prosperity of the region as a whole. The latent strength of the population and natural resources would inevitably attract undesirable external influences as has happened in the past. There may be comfort for some critics in the removal of what they see as a strategic threat, but there are always currents moving to fill power vacuums. It is impossible for Australia to control, or even predict them. . . . Living with a giant has its difficulties, but there are real advantages to offset them: the 'buffer' concept and unparalleled new trading opportunities are two of the most obvious. A power of Indonesia's size would also tend to attract to the region a prestige and world interest far greater than Australia and her other small neighbors could hope for. At Government level, Australia and Indonesia have maintained a degree of cordiality in their relationships which many other nations find extraordinary in the circumstances. It is based on a long-standing reservoir of goodwill and a realization of mutual interests. In the long term, it is the only realistic approach.

The Australian
Nov. 29, 1965.

AUSTRALIA'S LABOR GOVERNMENT in 1948 turned to strategic defense planning for Southeast Asia and the Southwest Pacific, since events had given urgency to the problem. The activities of Communist guerrillas in Malaya had created what was officially termed the "Emergency," which put a severe strain on the British and on the government of Malaya for a decade. Some 35,000 British soldiers and several air force units, plus numerous special police and constables, were mobilized to suppress the guerrillas. In May, 1948, the Australian government decided that if the British requested them, arms would be sent to Malaya.

On May 30, 1950, not many months after the Liberal-Country coalition came to power, Prime Minister Menzies discussed the problem of Malaya in Parliament, describing the Malayan situation as serious and as having deteriorated in the last few months. "Events in Malaya," he said, "are, of course, part of the global pattern of imperialistic communist oppression, and must be seen in the world context. . . . As shown by our experience in the recent war, Australia has a vital interest in the present situation in the Malay Peninsula, because of the relation of inescapable geographic and strategic facts, of its security. . . . Malaya is a key point in the strategic region, of which Australia is a main support area." While the defense of Malaya was the responsibility of the United Kingdom government, it was also a part of the regional defense problems in the Pacific that had to be shared by Australia, the United Kingdom, and other countries with interests in the area. Apart from the role that Australia might assume as a member of the Commonwealth in defense cooperation, it was fundamental to her security that the situation in Malaya be "cleared up as soon as possible." The government therefore was "giving careful consideration to the question of ways and means of assisting the

NEPAL

New Delhi

SIKKIM

BHUTAN

Peking

Seo

INDIA

CHINA

EAST PAKISTAN

BURMA

TAIWAN

Taipe

Rangoon

Vientiane

Hanoi

HONG KONG

THAILAND

LAOS

Manila

CEYLON

Bangkok

VIETNAM

Colombo

Saigon

PHILIPPINES

Phnom

Penh

CAMBODIA

MALAYSIA

BRUNEI

Kuala Lumpur

SINGAPORE

INDONESIA

Djakarta

TIMOR

Cocos Keeling Islands
(Australia)

North West Cape

Australia
and Its
Neighbors

Perth

KOREA JAPAN
Tokyo

MIDWAY

UNITED STATES

PACIFIC

WAKE ISLAND

ISLANDS

GUAM

TRUST

TERRITORY

GILBERT

New Guinea Trust Territory

Nauru
(Australia)
Trust Territory

Manus Island

(Australia)

SOLOMON ISLANDS

and

Papua
(Australia)

ELLICE ISLANDS

Darwin

NEW HEBRIDES

NEW CALEDONIA

FIJI

AUSTRALIA

Brisbane

Norfolk Island
• (Australia)

TONGA

Adelaide

Sydney

Lord Howe Island
(Australia)

Canberra

Melbourne

Hobart

NEW ZEALAND

Wellington

United Kingdom Government in the Malayan problem."[1]

The next day Menzies announced that the government of the United Kingdom had requested assistance in Malaya in the form of aircraft and crews and servicing for aircraft of the Royal Air Force stationed in the Far East. His government had agreed to provide a transport squadron of Dakota aircraft for supply dropping and general transport services. Crews and ground staff would total about 168. Probably with the object of forestalling the opposition's criticism, Menzies quoted a statement by Evatt on June 19, 1946, with which the government was in "full accord:" "As a principal power and member of the British Commonwealth in the Pacific, we must . . . be prepared to shoulder greater responsibilities for the defense of that area." Menzies quoted approvingly the words that Evatt reported he had spoken at the conference of prime ministers from which he had just returned; "and I am quite certain that I was expressing the sentiment of both sides of the House and the people of Australia . . . that it was recognized that Australia must in the future make a larger contribution towards the defence of the British Commonwealth."[2]

With this, matters rested until 1955. After a tour abroad and a two-day session with his cabinet to consider discussions he had conducted with American and British political leaders, Menzies made an important statement on April 1. The world, he said, was "full of danger. . . . China, which we, perhaps, once regarded as an ancient and inactive country is in course of becoming a great power under the sternest Communist control. Its armed manpower is enormous. Chinese Communism has in at least one vital respect followed the Russian course. It seeks to expand, to divide, and to conquer." The countries of Southeast Asia were under constant Chinese pressure from within and without. Did any Australian believe that his country's security would not

[1] *Current Notes*, XXI, 353-54.
[2] *Current Notes*, XXI, 354-55.

be seriously challenged "if the Communists overran South East Asia, subverted Indonesia and stood at the very threshold of our northern door?" He called upon all Australians to realize the basic truth that their country cannot be defended around the shores of Australia, "but if there is to be a war for our existence, it should be carried on as far from our shore as possible. It would be a sorry day for the security of Australia if we were driven to defend ourselves on our own soil; for that would connote the most disastrous defeats abroad and the most incredible difficulties for our friends and allies desiring to help us."[3]

Menzies said that Australia could neither defend itself by its own efforts within its own borders nor by resolutions of the "United Nations rendered impotent by the Communist veto." Australia could not "survive a surging Communist challenge from abroad except by the cooperation of powerful friends, including in particular the United Kingdom and the United States." Moreover, "If the battle against Communism is to be an effective one it must be as far north of Australia as possible." But Australia could not expect the collaboration of her friends and allies in "a comprehensive defence against aggressive Communism unless it was prepared to take its share of the responsibilities. Hence, if Malaya is vital to our defence, more vital properly understood, than some point on the Australian coast, then we must make Malayan defence in a real sense our business." In pursuing these views the government would establish naval, armed, and air forces in Malaya as part of a larger joint reserve. Menzies acknowledged these were not "massive forces," but "taken in conjunction with forces to be provided by our sister countries, they will be some proof of the seriousness with which we take the Communist threat and will, I have no doubt, serve as some guarantee to the people of Malaya that their present orderly progress towards demo-

[3] *Current Notes*, XXVI, 278-80.

cratic self-government, a progress which enjoys the deeply sympathetic interest of Australia, will not be interfered with by dictatorial Communist aggression."

Menzies' statement is a very important document of Australian foreign and defense policy, for, in effect, it constitutes the basis of the Menzies-Holt policy regarding Southeast Asia, and it attempts to give a reasoned justification for the policy. On June 16, Menzies announced that the forces to be sent to Malaya would be "available for use in operations against Communist terrorists," but their employment would not be permitted "in relation to any civil disturbance or in the internal affairs of the Federation or Singapore,"[4] and on July 4 the government declared that Australian troops would not be used "anywhere in Southeast Asia."[5] These clarifying statements were undoubtedly made to meet the sharp attacks of the opposition.

The decision to send troops to Malaya to help fight the Communist guerrillas was bitterly attacked by the opposition. In the platform adopted at its Conference in Hobart in February the Labor party declared that it was opposed to the "use of armed forces in Malaya," that the "use of Australian armed forces in Malaya will gravely injure Australian relations with our Asian neighbors while in no way contributing to the prevention of aggression." Calwell in a broadcast in June said that the Australian troops in Malaya would be engaged in a colonial expedition. Menzies' answer to this type of charge was, "We are anxious to see self-government established in Malaya at the earliest possible moment, and to that end we are ready to assist the peoples of Malaya to resist Communist bandits."[6]

Evatt suggested that Australia send a delegation to assist in peaceful negotiations with the terrorists. Casey regarded this suggestion as "insulting to the authorities and the people

[4] *Current Notes*, XXVI, 419.
[5] Apparently, Menzies did not consider Malaya as being in Southeast Asia.
[6] Statement of June 16, 1955, *Current Notes*, XXVI, 419.

of Malaya," for it tended "to equate the Communist bandits
with the leaders of the Malayan political parties," when "in
fact the terrorists were a few thousands in a population
of millions and had absolutely no claim to the exalted status
which Dr. Evatt was anxious to confer upon them. . . . Continued misrepresentation of the role of the Australian troops,"
Casey said, "could have a harmful effect in the Federation of
Malaya. One would almost think that Dr. Evatt and Mr.
Calwell, having falsely built up a picture of opposition in
Malaya to our troops, were now trying to make it come
true by stirring up suspicion of our motives."[7]

The debate about the commitment of troops to Malaya,
which took place in Parliament in April and May, was extremely bitter; one member characterized it as "the sharpest
clash on foreign policy since the conscription debate of
1916."[8] Evatt asserted that the stationing of troops in Malaya
could be interpreted as interference in the internal affairs of
Malaya and as an act of aggression. He charged that it was
an attempt to bolster imperialism in Southeast Asia; that it
could create "a beachhead for a new phase of colonialism."
Significantly, some years later Sukarno used this language
in his confrontation of Malaysia. The Labor leaders implied
that there was opposition in Malaya to the stationing of
troops there, but they produced no evidence to prove this.
Other critics contended that Asian problems could not be
solved by western intervention; they could be solved only
by Asians in Asian ways.[9] Sukarno and Subandrio also used
this language at a later date.

Other critics of the decision to send troops to Malaya
argued that the government's foreign policy reflected an
insistence upon defensive military alliances rather than a

[7] Broadcast by Casey on June 20. *Current Notes*, XXVI, 420.
[8] Statement by Allan Fraser, quoted in Greenwood and Harper, *Australia
in World Affairs, 1950-1955*, 190.
[9] Allan Fraser, quoted in Greenwood and Harper, *Australia in World
Affairs, 1950-1955*, 191.

recognition of the spirit of the United Nations Charter. Moreover, the decision was made without consulting the SEATO powers, and since the decision was made in the wrong way, it could not be right.[10] Evatt claimed in March, 1956, that the Australian public generally had accepted the Labor party's view that the employment of armed forces in Malaya was a "blunder."

JUST AS AUSTRALIA was hoping to recover the ground it had lost in Indonesia by its long support of the Dutch in the West New Guinea dispute, President Sukarno directed a confrontation against Malaysia. Having successfully removed the Dutch from Southeast Asia, he now was determined to remove the British.

As the colonial power, Great Britain was responsible for the defense and internal security of Malaya before it became independent in 1957. At that time Britain entered into a defense agreement with Malaya under which it assumed commitments for the defense of its former dependency. Australia was not a party to the agreement, but it became associated with it by an exchange of letters in 1959.[11]

Malaysia came into existence on September 16, 1963, by the incorporation of Singapore, Sarawak, and North Borneo with the Federation of Malaya. When the federation was formed in 1957, Singapore was left out for reasons which become obvious from an examination of the racial composition of the two. The population of the Federation was 50 percent Malaysian, 37 percent Chinese, and 13 percent others, chiefly Indians; while Singapore's population was 75 percent Chinese, 14 percent Malaysian, and 11 percent others, again mostly Indians. With Singapore out of the federation the Malaysians constituted only a bare half of

[10] R. W. Holt, March 8, 1956, *CPD*, House, IX, 661.
[11] Statement by Sir Garfield Barwick to House of Representatives, March 27, 1963. This arrangement has become generally known as ANZAM.

the population, but with Singapore added the Chinese out-
numbered the Malaysians by 100,000 or more. The two
racial groups, not even considering the more than one million Indians, differ in language, religion, customs, and economic interests. The literacy rate is highest among the Indians and lowest among the Malays. While the Malays are
chiefly rice growers, fishermen, and smallholder producers
of rubber, the Indians and Chinese dominate the commercial
and professional life—and many have been wage earners.

With Singapore excluded the Malays could dominate the
politics of the federation, unless sharp divisions should arise
among them. Many of the Chinese were not citizens and
therefore could not vote, but each year the percentage of
Malaya-born Chinese increased, thus narrowing the margin
of the Malayan advantage. There would be obvious economic advantages in having Singapore, a great financial,
commercial, and rapidly advancing industrial center, and
one of the great ports of the world, included in a federation,
but from the Malay point of view including it would involve great dangers. It might threaten Malay political control, even while the Malays were still far behind the Chinese
and the Indians in social and economic development. Moreover, there is a marked leftist trend in the politics of the
Chinese of Singapore.

The Malay leaders thus faced a dilemma: would Singapore constitute a greater menace inside or outside of a
federation? At the time of the formation of the federation in
1957 they apparently thought that Singapore outside would
prove less of a problem, but in 1961 they changed their
minds. Singapore would soon become independent, and its
prevailing political sentiment was strongly leftist. There
was a real fear that Singapore might support Chinese Communism. The federation's prime minister, Tengku Abdul
Rahman, fearing the development of a "Chinese Cuba,"
seems to have decided that the best way to meet this danger
was to incorporate Singapore into the federation. Radicalism

in the city-island could be better controlled with Singapore as a component part of a federation than as a foreign state which might turn to Communist China. To neutralize the huge increase in the number of Chinese in the expanded federation, Rahman suggested the simultaneous incorporation of the three British dependencies in North Borneo—Sarawak, Brunei, and Sabah (North Borneo). With the inclusion of all of these territories, the percentage of Chinese in the total population would be reduced somewhat, but, unfortunately for the Malays, it would increase the percentage of non-Malays. If in the future the non-Malays should unite on political issues, the Malays might become dissatisfied and might consider union with Indonesia as a means of controlling the Chinese and other non-Malays.

Most nations were pleased with the formation of the Federation of Malaysia, except Indonesia and the Philippines, two countries with which Australia was especially desirous of developing friendly relations. The British were glad to get rid of some troublesome remainders of the Empire, and most of the world supported the further liquidation of colonialism. The Filipinos, chiefly President Diosdado Macapagal and his strongest supporters, advanced a claim to parts of Sabah, based upon alleged rights of suzerainty of the sultan of Sulu, while Indonesia objected to the incorporation of the North Borneo territories in the Malaysian Federation on the basis that it represented neocolonialism and was a violation of the principles of a new regional organization, Maphilindo, which had been organized by Malaya, the Philippines, and Indonesia on the eve of the creation of the Federation of Malaysia.

Indonesia at first did not oppose the inclusion of Sarawak and Sabah in the enlarged federation. Subandrio told the General Assembly of the United Nations that "when Malaya told us of her intentions to merge with the three British Crown colonies of Sarawak, Brunei and British North Borneo as one Federation, we told them that we have no objections and that we wish them success with this merger so that everyone may live in peace and freedom." It was evident from the following passage in Subandrio's speech, however, that the Indonesian leaders were not really pleased: "Naturally, ethnologically and geographically speaking, this British part is closer to Indonesia than, let us say, to Malaya. But we still told Malaya that we have no objections to such a merger based upon the will for freedom of the peoples concerned."[12]

The revolt of Brunei in December, 1962, may have changed Indonesia's attitude. A number of rebels received military training in Indonesian Borneo, and the leader, A. M. A. Azahari, had served in the Indonesian army. He denounced the proposed Federation of Malaysia as a device to make Brunei a colony of Malaya.[13] When the revolt broke out, he was in Manila. British troops from Singapore put down the revolt. Since Brunei was a protectorate and not a colony, the British government left to the sultan the decision as to whether or not his state should join the federation. Reluctance to share the rich oil revenues of his state with the proposed federation and difficulties over the question of his eligibility to become the paramount ruler influenced the sultan's decision not to join.

The Indonesian government developed a panoply of arguments to justify its opposition to the Federation of Malaysia. It charged that the expanded federation was a neocolonialist plot, that its purpose was to encircle Indonesia, that Malaya had always been hostile to Indonesia and had tried to annex Sumatra during the revolt of 1957-1958, that Malaysia would be used as a base for foreign domination of Indonesia and

[12] The writers have been unable to find this statement in the official documents of the United Nations, but it is quoted in *A Survey of the Controversial Problem of the Establishment of the Federation of Malaysia,* published and distributed by the Information Division, Embassy of Indonesia (Washington, no date), 2.

[13] See Bruce Grant, *Indonesia* (Melbourne, 1964), 142, for the relations of Azahari with Indonesia.

as a "haven for the economic subversion of Indonesia," and that the Federation of Malaysia was opposed to the "Revolution of Mankind" and the "New Emerging Forces."[14] Privately, Indonesian leaders said that they were opposed to Malaysia because it would facilitate Chinese infiltration into northern Borneo and prepare the way for a Chinese takeover of this strategic area. On the other hand, Rahman believed that incorporating these territories into Malaysia would prevent China from picking them off one by one.

There was little evidence to support the Indonesian charges. There were, it is true, profitable British investments in Malaya, and Malaya's large exports of rubber and tin were important foreign exchange earners. The treaty of defense between Great Britain and Malaya was extended to Malaysia, and Britain retained use of the military base on Singapore for "the defence of Malaysia and for Commonwealth defence and the preservation of peace in Southeast Asia." Likely, what most troubled Sukarno and his supporters was that Malaya was enjoying peace and prosperity —the highest per capita income of all the countries of South and Southeast Asia. This might have a dangerous attraction for deeply divided Indonesia, especially nearby Sumatra and Borneo. The fact that the British government had sent a commission, the Cobbold Commission, to ascertain the wishes of the peoples of Sarawak and Sabah concerning their territories joining Malaysia, and that the United Nations made a similar survey of sentiment for federation in these territories in August, 1963, and found it favorable, did not impress or discourage the Indonesian government.

[14] See statements by the Indonesian representative, Sudjarwo, to the United Nations Security Council in Sept., 1964, when that body considered the charges brought by Malaysia of the landing of Indonesian paratroopers in south Malaya. U.N. Security Council, *Official Records*, 1149th Meeting, Sept. 14, 1964. General Abdul Haris Nasution, defense minister and army chief of staff, told the armed forces: "Malaysia is a state under foreign control politically, economically and particularly, militarily. As a result it is becoming a base for foreign domination in Southeast Asia and for subverting our economy and security." *The New York Times*, Oct. 3, 1963.

During the summer months of 1963 there were numerous diplomatic attempts to bring the parties together and to arrive at a peaceful solution. Apparently Barwick was instrumental in these activities,[15] but to no avail.

AFTER A CABINET MEETING which reviewed progress toward the creation of Malaysia, Barwick issued a statement on March 5, 1963, that "Australia believes that the establishment of Malaysia would contribute to the stability of the region and that it deserves support as a major act of orderly decolonization. Territories with a common administrative background and currency and with close economic and political ties are uniting in independence."[16] When it was reported, apparently erroneously, that Rahman had said that Australia was committed militarily to the defense of Malaysia,[17] Barwick stated there was no military alliance with Malaysia. The Australian troops in Malaya were Australia's contribution to the Commonwealth strategic reserve stationed in Malaya by formal agreement between the United Kingdom and Malaya, but the security of Malaya was a direct concern of Australia.[18]

With the birth of Malaysia in September, 1963, Indonesia began to prepare a confrontation against Malaysia.[19] Mobs attacked and burned the British embassy and looted homes and property of English nationals. The situation became so disturbed that an airlift began removing British, Australian, and New Zealand children from the Djakarta area. Indonesia rejected the Federation of Malaysia, and the Philip-

---

15 J. F. Cairns, *Living With Asia* (Melbourne, 1965), 84. Cairns, a Labor member of Parliament, states that Barwick "played an active and favorably recognized part in these efforts."
16 *Current Notes*, XXXIV, 36.
17 *Sydney Morning Herald*, March 12, 1963.
18 *Courier Mail*, March 13, 1963.
19 On Sept. 2, General Nasution said that he believed his country had helped train "more than 6,000 anti-British, anti-Malaysia rebels in the Northern Borneo territories." *The New York Times*, Sept. 3, 1963.

pine government requested the reduction of its embassy in Kuala Lumpur to the status of a consulate, whereupon Prime Minister Rahman announced on September 16 that his government had severed diplomatic relations with the two states.[20] On September 20 the Indonesian government announced the takeover of all British companies in Indonesia, allegedly to insure safety and continued production.[21]

The Australian government quickly announced its support for Malaysia. Menzies informed the House of Representatives on September 17 that the provision in the British-Malaya defense agreement of 1957 creating the Far East Strategic Reserve (composed of British, Malaysian, Australian, and New Zealand troops), under which the Australian forces helped put down insurrectionary activities, would cover Malaysia.[22] Two days later Deputy Prime Minister McEwen stated that "we have made it perfectly clear that we support Malaysia. We are in no doubt that the entire Australian community supports Malaysia."[23]

On September 25, Menzies announced in Parliament that Australia would give military assistance to defend Malaysia "in the event of any armed invasion or of any subversive activity supported, directed, or inspired from outside Malaysia." He pointed out that as far back as 1955 the government had recognized the importance of Malaya to the security of the zone in which Australians lived and that "in consequence Malayan integrity and defence were matters from which we could not and should not stand aloof. . . . But Malaysia, the new nation, is here," he said. "The processes of its creation have been democratic. The United Nations secretary-general, having appointed suitable persons as examiners, reported that the people of North Borneo and Sarawak desired incorporation into Malaysia. . . . We

[20] *The New York Times*, Sept. 18, 1963.
[21] *The New York Times*, Sept. 21, 1963.
[22] *CPD*, House, XXXIX, 1027.
[23] *CPD*, House, XXXIX, 1257-58.

have publicly and unambiguously said that we support Malaysia, which is a Commonwealth country just as our own is."[24]

Calwell replied that the Labor party supported "the concept of Malaysia" and welcomed its creation. "We believe that this experiment in nationhood should be given its chance, free from attack or interference from other nations, to prove itself." He explained that the Labor party had repealed its plank calling for the withdrawal of troops from Malaysia, but it was insisting that "their continued presence in Malaysia shall be covered by a treaty, clear, open and, if possible, mutual, which gives Australia an effective voice in the decision of the treaty powers." He referred to the "shameful" West New Guinea episode, a repetition of which should be avoided. "In that case we misled the Netherlands and confused Indonesia. Both had cause to be doubtful of our attitude, and in the end both grew contemptuous of our ambiguity . . . we owe it to our neighbors to clarify our intentions by means of an open treaty."[25]

Menzies apparently had anticipated the opposition's response. He retorted that a treaty was unnecessary and might be harmful because it was restrictive. The government of Malaysia had said clearly that it was satisfied with an exchange of notes. "But it has not been the normal practice of Commonwealth countries to spell out in detail their sense of mutual obligation, nor to confine themselves to legal formulae. For example, our vital engagements with the United Kingdom are not written or in any way formalized. Yet we know and she knows that in this part of the world we look to her, and she to us. We each apply in a spirit of mutual confidence a golden rule of mutual obligation."[26]

The government's position was probably explained by its loyalty to Britain and its willingness to follow London's

[24] *CPD*, House, XL, 1338-39.
[25] *CPD*, House, XL, 1365-69.
[26] *CPD*, House, XL, 1338-39.

94   *Australia Faces Southeast Asia*

leadership. The Labor party's views may have stemmed
from a nationalistic spirit and a latent isolationism. A treaty
would very likely limit the commitment. Conceivably, a
"mutual" agreement such as the Labor party wanted might
even be impossible.

IN THE FALL of 1963, Parliament still had a year to go before
the next election, but on October 15, Menzies announced
to the House of Representatives that the government had
asked the governor-general to dissolve Parliament and call
for a general election. In justification of this action Menzies
said that other states concerned should know whether the
government's policy in support of Malaysia had the "clear
backing" of the Australian people. The opposition did not
support the government's policy, and the government had
an effective majority of only one vote in the House. He
believed that Australia's problems in the near neighborhood
were too critical to permit uncertainty in national policy,
and government with an effective mandate was imperative.

The Labor party leaders, who earlier had pressed for a
new election, were convinced that the government requested
a premature dissolution of Parliament because it believed
it could at this time win seats on the Malaysian issue.[27]
Menzies argued that the Labor party's position as stated by
Calwell, that the continued presence of Australian troops
in Malaysia should be covered by "a treaty, clear, open,
and if possible, mutual," did not constitute support of the
government's policy for two reasons. First, Malaysia was
not an "aligned" country and was not a party to SEATO.
"It is a matter of high policy for Malaysia to be regarded as
a nation jealous of its independence, but not as one having,
in peace-time at any rate, mutual contractual military obligations with any other country." The United Kingdom did

[27] See Cairns, *Living With Asia*, 89-90.

have a defense arrangement with Malaysia, but this was because Great Britain was the colonial power and felt it had an obligation to give effective assurances to the new nation that its complete independence would be preserved. Australia stood in a different position. If what the opposition wanted was "that there should be a mutual treaty of defence between Australia and Malaysia, under which Malaysia becomes our ally for military purposes in advance of any armed attack upon cooperating Australian forces, such a treaty would, in the absence of a revolutionary change of Malaysian policy, be impossible of achievement." Secondly, the government believed that the opposition's proposal was impractical and that Australia would be at a disadvantage if her help were conditioned by a detailed treaty. It was better to have a simple, clear declaration of intention, which by its nature "preserves our judgment as to the nature, extent, and disposition of Australian forces to be deployed."

Calwell's reply to Menzies' statement was brief and equivocal. A Labor government, he said, would immediately go to the aid of Malaysia if it were attacked, even without a treaty, although a treaty would be concluded.[28]

The government fought the election on three foreign and defense policy issues: (1) Australia's commitment to Malaysia, (2) the agreement with the United States for the establishment of a naval communications base in northwest Australia, and (3) the Labor party's proposal for a nuclear-free zone south of the equator. In the election, which was held November 30, 1963, the government coalition gained seven seats. At the opening of Parliament the following February, the government declared that it would continue to support the political and territorial integrity of Malaysia. "In addition to its pledge to provide forces if necessary to assist Malaysia and Great Britain in the defence of Malaysia

[28] *Keesing's Contemporary Archives,* 1963-1964, p. 19825.

against externally directed aggression and insurgency," it was assisting the development of Malaysia's own defense forces. The government declared that it was "deeply concerned" about relations with Indonesia, and its policy toward that country would continue to be one "of friendship, pursued with patience, frankness and realism. The major interest which we have in common should, if possible, be preserved," but the government emphasized to Indonesia that "we have commitments in relation to Malaysia which we will honor."[29]

A STRANGE SITUATION had developed between Australia and Indonesia. There were Australian troops in Sarawak and Sabah facing Indonesian troops across the border in Borneo. By March, 1964, there were several hundred infiltrators from Indonesia in Sarawak and Sabah. While Australia had publicly, through diplomatic channels, and by direct communication made clear its support of Malaysia and its disapproval of Indonesia's policies, it declared that its policy toward Indonesia would continue to be one "of seeking to promote sound and friendly relations" though "without sacrifice of Australian vital interests."[30] Indonesia obviously also was careful not to exacerbate tensions between the two countries. In spite of Australia's complete support of Britain and Malaysia in the controversy, the Indonesian government tempered its words and its actions toward Australia. While the British embassy was attacked there were no anti-Australian demonstrations or attacks on the Australian embassy.

Australian leaders were deeply concerned about the United States' position in the Malaysian affair, which seemed to be one of "cordial noninvolvement." The United States was becoming more deeply involved in Vietnam and wished to

[29] *CPD*, House, XLI, 10-11.
[30] Minister of External Affairs Barwick, March 11, 1964, *CPD*, House, XLI, 480.

limit its military commitments in Southeast Asia. It regarded the conflict with Indonesia primarily as the responsibility of Great Britain and the Commonwealth. Moreover, Washington was in a quandary. Its strategy was to back General Nasution and the Indonesian army as a counterweight against the Communists, but this army now was engaged in an effort to crush Malaysia, and the United States was sympathetic with the formation of Malaysia.

Not surprisingly, Australian leaders were worried at this time. Sukarno was intensifying his threat. On May 3, 1964, he issued an "action command" to "21 million volunteers" in the fight to crush Malaysia. He urged the volunteers to help the various peoples of Malaysia to win "national independence." In a speech to 400,000 people, Sukarno repeated a statement he had made three weeks before to the American ambassador, that the United States could "go to hell" with its economic aid. The day before, Defense Minister General Nasution told a press conference that Indonesia was giving "concrete aid" to guerrillas in Malaysian Borneo. "We are training them and President Sukarno has even ordered us to mobilize our volunteers to fight together with the North Kalimantan [Borneo] fighters to wipe out the British neo-colonialist plot," he was reported to have said.[31] Some weeks before, Subandrio had warned Australia that "the responsibility for any war must be plainly placed on Australian shoulders and it certainly will not be a local war." Probably to point up Subandrio's warning, the chairman of Parliament said that two divisions of Communist North Korean "volunteers" would join Indonesia's "volunteers to crush Malaysia."[32] At this time the Indonesian ambassador to Australia advised Canberra not to "interfere" in Malaysia, which he described as "an Asian problem, to be solved by Asians in an Asian atmosphere and in an Asian way."[33]

31 *The New York Times*, May 4, 1964.
32 *The New York Times*, April 20, 1964.
33 *Melbourne Age*, April 8, 1964.

Upon his return from a visit to Washington where he conferred with the Secretary of State, Barwick suggested strongly that the United States would regard any attack on Australian forces in Borneo as coming within the scope of the ANZUS treaty.[34] This statement led to a sharp exchange of words in Parliament. A member asked whether in making this statement, Barwick was expressing his own opinion or the joint opinion of the governments of Australia and the United States. To this, Barwick replied that "an attack on armed forces of a party is within the treaty if the attack takes place in the treaty area. . . . Borneo is in the treaty area. On that point there is no difference whatever."[35]

Calwell differed sharply with Barwick, saying that he had been informed by Under Secretary of State Averell Harriman that the American government did believe that the ANZUS commitment included Australian troops already in Malaysia. However, the opposition leader pointed out those troops were there "long before the creation of Malaysia and they are still there to serve an objective which comes completely within the ambit of American policy, namely, the strategy of containment of Communism. To suggest, as the minister has done, that unilateral action by Australia in pursuit of an entirely different object, carries the same obligation on America's part is highly contentious, to say the least. . . . To put it quite bluntly, the American government just does not see the Malaysian dispute as coming under ANZUS, or even involving it, even though two of the signatories, ourselves and New Zealand, have given quite different commitments to Malaysia." He charged Sir Garfield with refusing to state whether he had a specific undertaking from the United States and with basing his case on interpretation alone. The government was also accused of trying to involve the United States in the Malaysian affair.

In the midst of the controversy and just as Sir Garfield

---

[34] *Sydney Sunday Herald*, April 19, 1964.
[35] April 21, 1964, *CPD*, House, XLII, 1235.

was on the point of leaving on a six-weeks diplomatic mission, the cabinet unexpectedly appointed him the chief justice of the High Court.[36] He was succeeded by Minister of Defense Paul Hasluck, who generally was regarded as having a firmer attitude toward Indonesia.

When Under Secretary of State Averell Harriman was in Australia in June, he gave assurance that the United States would defend Australian-administered East New Guinea if it were attacked.[37] This obviously was not nearly the commitment which Barwick claimed had been accepted by the United States under the ANZUS treaty.

Australians were unhappy about the attitude of the United States government. In a visit to Australia in 1963, Secretary of State Rusk had urged Australians to take a more active part in the defense of the free world, but it now seemed that the United States was only concerned with major cold-war issues and that conflicts outside the East-West confrontation were mere "embarrassments." "China in United States' eyes is the one and only Asian danger," wrote the *Sydney Daily Telegraph*.[38] "Indonesia is seen almost as a benevolent power, or at least one to be treated with the utmost tact. In forming a policy we cannot delude ourselves that we can rely on American protection in any conflict that does not involve a direct Communist threat."

In his effort to get wider support for the defense of Malaysia, Menzies visited Washington in June, 1964, and tried to discourage the United States from continuing to train Indonesian military officers. He also sought direct aid for Malaysia and a clarification of American commitments under the ANZUS treaty. The treaty is somewhat ambiguous on this point. Article IV states that "each Party recognizes that an armed attack on any of the Parties would be danger-

[36] *The New York Times*, April 24, 1964.
[37] *The New York Times*, June 4, 1963.
[38] Feb. 28, 1963.

ous to its own peace and safety and declares that it would act to meet the common danger in accordance with its constitutional processes," and Article V says that "an armed attack on any of the Parties is deemed to include an armed attack on the metropolitan territory of any of the Parties, or on the island territories under its jurisdiction in the Pacific or on its armed forces, public vessels or aircraft in the Pacific." Did this cover Australian troops in Sabah and Sarawak? The position of the United States government seemed to be that it did, provided they were not in a combat role when attacked.

The question of the point at which the ANZUS treaty placed an obligation on the United States to help its allies was also discussed at the annual meeting of the ANZUS Council, which was held in Washington on July 17 and 18, 1964. The United States government had affirmed diplomatically to British and other Commonwealth leaders that it was committed to the survival of Malaysia, but the Australians wanted stronger public statements of support for Malaysia and warnings to Indonesia. The paragraph on Malaysia in the Council's communique was carefully and mildly worded. While the Council affirmed its support of Malaysia, Indonesia was not labeled an aggressor, or even mentioned by name.[39]

Menzies apparently had had difficulty in getting a satisfactory resolution of support for Malaysia from the Commonwealth Prime Ministers' Conference, which met in London just prior to the ANZUS Council meeting, held in Washington. Some of the prime ministers believed much could be

[39] The paragraph reads as follows: "The Council affirmed its continuous support for Malaysia. It noted that two of its members are now giving aid, both in forces and material, to assist Malaysian defence. The Council recognized that in this region, as elsewhere, force must not be employed in violation of the territorial integrity of other nations. It espoused the hope that the independence of Malaysia would be respected and that peaceful relationships with neighboring states would be restored so that all could contribute to the peace, security and advancement of Southeast Asia and the South and West Pacific." *Current Notes,* XXXV, 40-41.

achieved by direct negotiations with Sukarno or by negotiations of a general nature; others said their countries were in no position to give Malaysia material aid. Sir Robert argued that while only some members would find it within their power to give military aid, all should give at least moral aid to Malaysia. The prime ministers "assured the Prime Minister of Malaysia of their sympathy and support in his efforts to preserve the sovereign independence and integrity of his country." There was considerable discussion of the word "support." It was agreed that support could be moral, diplomatic, or military.[40]

WITH THE BREAKDOWN of the summit conference of Prime Minister Rahman, President Sukarno, and President Macapagal of the Philippines, which met in Tokyo on June 20, 1964, Indonesia began to increase the pressure on Malaysia. Heretofore, after each failure of negotiations, hostile activities against Sarawak and Sabah were increased, but this time Indonesia began paratroop and naval landings in the Malay Peninsula. On September 3, Malaysia, in a letter to the president of the Security Council of the United Nations, charged Indonesia with "blatant and inexcusable aggression" and requested that the president call an "urgent" meeting to consider the matter. Confronted with the evidence, the Indonesian representative did not deny the charge before the Council, but claimed that Indonesia's actions were natural and wholly justified.[41] A mild resolution, proposed by Norway, calling upon the parties "to refrain from all threat or use of force to respect the territorial integrity and political independence of each other" and recommending that the parties "resume their talks," received nine votes and Russia's veto.

[40] See broadcast by Menzies, *Current Notes,* XXXV, 32ff.
[41] The Security Council held six meetings on the case from Sept. 3 to 17, 1964. For the verbatim records of the meetings see U.N. Security Council, *Official Records,* 1144th, 1145th, 1148th to 1150th, 1152nd meetings.

As external affairs minister, Barwick consistently had minimized the verbal attacks of Indonesian leaders and chided as alarmists those who took President Sukarno's proclamations seriously and the Indonesian arms buildup as threatening to Australian security. This concurred with Australia's desire to maintain normal relations with Indonesia—to treat it as a friend in need. The government, however, took a steadily more serious view of the matter. After the landing of paratroops on the peninsula and the failure of the Security Council even to censure Indonesia, it decided upon stern measures. In November, 1964, it stopped training Indonesian military officers. The government's increasing concern about developments in the north—in Vietnam as well as in Malaysia—was indicated by an announcement on November 10, 1964, by Menzies of a new defense policy. Conscription would be resumed in 1965, with a callup of 4,200 men and 6,900 in 1966 and 1967, respectively. Conscripted men would be liable to serve overseas. Defense expenditures would rise from £A260,500,000 in 1963-1964 to £A429,100,000 in 1967-1968. Two existing airfields in New Guinea were to be improved, and a third built.[42]

In October, 1964, for the first time, Australian troops were in actual combat against the Indonesians when the Indonesians made a raid near Malacca. Despite all these developments, the desire to maintain normal relations with Indonesia, to treat it as a friend in need, persisted. It was generally agreed that all nonmilitary exchanges should be continued, that communications should be kept open, for "we are neighbors." Even after Indonesia withdrew from the United Nations on January 10, 1965, Australia continued to give it economic aid.

While trying to maintain friendship with Indonesia, Australia was becoming more deeply involved in the defense of Malaysia against Indonesian aggression. On February 3,

[42] *CPD*, House, XLIV, 2715-24.

1965, McEwen announced that Australia's battalion of infantry was being moved from Malaya, where it had been used against Communists and guerrillas, to North Borneo, where it would serve in rotation with British and Malaysian troops. Some Indonesian reactions to Australia's increased military action now became evident. Indonesia's Provisional Peoples Consultative Assembly associated Australia with the "imperialists" and recommended measures of reprisal against Australian interests in Indonesia. Sukarno on April 18, in a speech at the tenth anniversary meeting of the Asian-African Conference in Bandung, made some threatening remarks directed at Australia: "To our East, too, in Oceana the people must be given their chance to become masters in their own homes and manage their own affairs."[43] Did this mean that Australian New Guinea would be hit with subversion and infiltration, or was the implied threat made to discourage further Australian aid to Malaysia?

Whatever Sukarno's intention, his statements were not likely to cause Australians to slacken their support of Malaysia. The *Hobart Mercury* probably expressed the predominant sentiment among Australian people when it wrote that "the time could be close when Australia will have to choose between a doubtful friendship and letting Indonesia know in no uncertain fashion that her behavior cannot be tolerated. Indonesia got away with it in West New Guinea. She could be aiming to repeat the performance elsewhere. In that case she is due for a shock, and there should be no hesitation in administering it."[44] The *Sydney Morning Herald* was critical of the government's lack of determined response to this imminently dangerous situation. "There is no quickening of the tempo of defence preparations, no expansion of the small and leisurely defence programme, no government call to the nation to prepare to meet an emergency. Instead,

[43] Quoted by T. B. Millar, "Problems of Australian Foreign Policy, Jan. to June, 1965," *Australian Journal of Politics and History*, X, 267ff.
[44] Jan. 29, 1963.

Canberra gives the appearance of trying to 'play down' the crisis. . . . Political prudence as well as national responsibility should influence the government to grasp the nettle and order all necessary measures to build up, urgently, an adequate structure of defence."[45]

In mid-January, 1965, the Federal Parliamentary Executive of the Labor party issued a policy statement on Malaysia with which Liberals could find little to disagree. "The action taken by Australia to assist Malaysia's defence up to this point is justified," the statement said. "Not only should the Australian government make continuously plain to Indonesia its determination to resist aggression in this area; it should also be outspoken (1) in deploring Indonesian withdrawal from the United Nations and in persuading Indonesia to reconsideration of that ill-fated decision; (2) in condemning reckless provocations in speech and action by Indonesian leaders as have brought about the burning of embassies and other outrages against civilized behavior in Djakarta."[46] However, Labor still demanded a treaty regulating aid to Malaysia.

Australia, and also the United States, Great Britain, and the non-Communist countries of Southeast Asia, had reason to be increasingly concerned in 1965, because Sukarno was steering his country into alignment with Communist China, and in his Merdeka [Independence] Day speech on August 17 he proclaimed a new "anti-imperialism axis" of Indonesia, Communist China, North Korea, North Vietnam, and Cambodia. Within its borders he was pushing his country toward Marhaenism, the Sukarno version of Marxist socialism. These

[45] Sept. 15, 1964. In the early days of confrontation there was an occasional critical voice like that of the political commentator, Douglas Wilkie, who questioned the Australian policy: "The rights of Indonesia are the rights of any great nation of 100 million people to be consulted about the disposal of strategically vital territories on its borders. . . . Far from consulting Indonesia or the Philippines, it [the British government] did not even invite Australia to take part in a major-political decision on Australia's own doorstep." *Melbourne Sun and Sydney Mirror*, Feb. 13, 1963.

[46] See Millar, *Australian Journal of Politics and History*, XI, 267ff.

movements placed the large Indonesian Communist party in a more favorable and influential position.[47] About this time Djakarta hinted that Indonesia soon would have an atomic bomb, apparently with the promised help of Peking.[48]

Sukarno's object in forging the axis with Communist China was obvious. Djakarta and Peking both were desirous of getting Great Britain and the United States out of Southeast Asia, and they resorted to this outflanking maneuver in the hope of getting Singapore, which had just been thrust out of the Federation of Malaysia, to deny the British the further use of a military base on the island. How Sukarno planned to deal with the situation after the two great western powers had been pushed out of the region and Communist China could move into it at will can only be conjectured.

These ominous developments made it difficult for Menzies to act and speak as if Australia and Indonesia were on friendly terms. At a press conference in July, 1965, Sir Robert said that Australian and Indonesian soldiers, facing each other, were engaged in actions similar to "operations of war." This remark apparently caused some diplomatic perturbation, although the Australian newspapers gave it little attention. A Labor member of the House inquired whether an interview had taken place between the Indonesian ambassador and the secretary of the External Affairs Department at which Indonesia was assured that a state of war did not exist between the two countries. If such assurance was given, he asked, why was it necessary to do so?[49] According to the press, the Indonesian ambassador, after a careful scrutiny of the text of Menzies' press conference and a meeting with the secretary of the External Affairs Department, reported to Djakarta that Menzies' remarks did not mean a change of policy. He concluded that Sir Robert's use

---

[47] See dispatches by Seymour Topping in *The New York Times*, Aug. 22 and 25, 1965.

[48] Topping, *The New York Times*, Aug. 25, 1965.

[49] *The Age*, Aug. 18, 1965.

of the phrase "operations of war" was ambiguous.[50] Later, at an Indonesian reception to celebrate its twentieth anniversary as a republic, Hasluck proposed a toast to Sukarno, and the Indonesian ambassador proposed a toast to the Queen.[51]

With the expulsion of Singapore from the Federation, which was announced on August 9, the situation had changed markedly, and Australians began to have second thoughts. Racial disharmony within the Federation of Malaysia was an even greater danger to its life than Indonesian confrontation. When voices were being raised in Sabah and Sarawak for a reconsideration of membership in the federation, Rahman said that they could not withdraw. Australians were especially alarmed by the statement of Singapore's Prime Minister Lee Kuan Yew that the British could be kicked out of the big military and naval base on twenty-four-hours' notice and that the Americans never would be allowed to take it over. Should the Americans enter Malaysia, he threatened, he would hand over the base to the Russians. Moreover, Lee reproached Menzies and his government for not doing more to help hold Malaysia together. Australia had a strong interest in keeping Malaysia intact, but, as the September 1, 1965, *Melbourne Age* observed, "What more could they [Menzies and his government] have done without an unwarranted interference in another country's affairs is a riddle that Mr. Lee is not prepared to answer."

WITH THE ABORTIVE Communist-supported coup on September 30, 1965, the Indonesian situation changed suddenly. The new government, dominated by the army, wanted to end the costly confrontation and to concentrate on solving the country's serious economic problems. Sukarno, whose power was curbed only gradually, wanted to continue the confrontation policy, but after his forced transfer of executive powers to General Suharto in March, 1966, the new foreign minister, Adam Malik, pressed negotiations with Malaysia for a peace treaty. The treaty, which was signed on August 11, 1966, formally ended the confrontation, but Malaysia agreed to give the people of Sarawak and Sabah the opportunity "to reaffirm as soon as practicable in a free and democratic manner through general elections their previous decision about their status in Malaysia."[52] After an August visit to Djakarta by Hasluck, Indonesian Foreign Minister Malik said that Australian-Indonesian relations had "cleared up."[53]

This brought to an end the ambivalent relations which existed between the two countries during the confrontation. "Australia's policy was one of trying to graduate its response to Indonesian provocation in Malaysia and to isolate this aspect of our relations."[54] Indonesia responded in somewhat the same manner, probably in gratitude to Australia for help in its struggle for independence. Was the Australian policy successful? British, Australian, and New Zealand support of Malaysia deprived Sukarno of an easy victory, but confrontation was ended not by the pressure exerted by the Commonwealth countries but by an internal eruption in Indonesia. Moreover, the problem of Singapore has not been solved, but now has become a separate problem.[55] Nevertheless, Australia demonstrated firmness in resisting aggression in Southeast Asia, apparently without any permanent impairment of its relations with Indonesia.

[52] *The New York Times,* Aug. 14, 1966.
[53] *News and Views,* Consulate General of the Republic of Indonesia, Aug. 2, 1966.
[54] Shane Paltridge, "Australia and the Defense of Southeast Asia," *Foreign Affairs,* XLIV, Oct. 1965, 56. Paltridge was minister for defense. The somewhat ambivalent attitude of Australia toward Indonesia is reflected in the new Australian embassy building in Djakarta, which has several security features such as a high spiked fence surrounding it and armored glass windows. It has been dubbed the "elegant fort."
[55] There remains the danger that Malay extremists may attempt some violence on Singapore, and the Singapore Chinese may resort to desperate measures to maintain their independence against the Malays.

6 *Peril to the North-- Vietnam*

There are various reasons why we should be afraid of the situation that is developing in Southeast Asia; one is population, another is poverty, another is racialism and religious feeling, and another is Communism and yet another is the ineffectiveness of the United Nations as a peace-keeping organization.

> IAN ALLEN
> House of Representatives
> March 23, 1965

We need to see the difference between a wish and a policy. We all wish for peace, prosperity, world understanding and the peaceful settlement of disputes. These are not policies but wishes. A policy is a planned course of conduct devised by a government to serve an identified purpose and put into effect by its own efforts. If it is put into effect by the efforts of others it is not a policy but a hope. If it is proclaimed but not associated with any measures of any kind for putting it into effect it is a piece of humbug.

> PAUL HASLUCK
> Minister for External Affairs
> Devonshire, Tasmania
> July 16, 1965

AUSTRALIANS LONG HAVE feared "aggression from the North." Before World War II it feared aggression from Japan, and, as a result of the frightening experiences in World War II when the Japanese advanced to the very threshold of their mainland, Australians for a long time held a deep-seated distrust of Japan. With the rise to power of the Communists on the mainland of China, the Australians' concern shifted to the "downward thrust of China" and the "advance of Communism."

It is significant that the Australian policy toward China began to diverge from that of Britain. The Liberal-Country government with Robert Menzies as prime minister normally would have preferred to follow and to support British foreign policy, but Australia was too concerned about the dangers to its security from the Red Chinese influence in the troubled world of Southeast Asia to follow London in recognizing the Communist Chinese regime. Significantly also, Canberra aligned itself with Washington in this matter, though not necessarily and certainly not exclusively to insure security.[1]

Under the circumstances it is not surprising that Australia soon began to give aid to South Vietnam, as part of the program for support of the Asian members of SEATO. This was emphasized by the government, probably to provide a legal justification for the assistance. In 1956 the Australian government made £A2,000,000 available for aid in support of the defense efforts of the SEATO members, and in 1958 another £A1,000,000. On May 7, 1962, Barwick announced

[1] See Henry S. Albinski, *Australia and the China Problem during the Korean War Period* (Canberra, 1964), 21. Albinski concludes that the decision not to recognize the Communist regime was the product of a number of factors: "the accidental conjunction of the 1949 election and the rather lengthy and unavoidable unpreparedness of the new government to reach a judgment on recognition; the advent of a distasteful Chinese behavior pattern immediately following Colombo . . .; the government's appreciation of disturbing events in Asia, for which China was held in part responsible; the pressing need to engage American support for an alliance."

the commitment of £A3,000,000 more, chiefly for South Vietnam, which had asked for aid under the Manila Treaty. This was in addition to £A500,000 which already had been committed for expenditure under the existing program of economic assistance. Sir Garfield said that in making these sums available the government wished "to emphasize the importance it placed on SEATO as the basis for concerted resistance to communist pressure in the treaty area."[2]

This announcement by Barwick was followed by another on May 24 by Minister of Defense A. G. Townley that thirty Australian army personnel would be sent to South Vietnam to provide "instruction in jungle warfare, village defence and other related activities such as engineering and signals. . . . There was in Vietnam," he stated, "an urgent problem of Communist infiltration and insurgency, fomented and directed by and supported from North Viet Nam." Some assistance already had been provided in the form of communications equipment, barbed wire, and other materials for village defense.[3] Barwick emphasized that Australia would not be providing combat forces, but he warned that if the Communists achieved their aims in Vietnam, "this would gravely affect the security of the whole South East-Asia area and ultimately Australia itself. The Australian government's response to the invitation to assist Viet Nam, which was a Protocol State under the SEATO Treaty was in accordance with Australia's obligations under that treaty."[4] Four days later he announced that at the invitation of the government of Thailand a squadron of RAAF Sabre jet fighter aircraft was being sent to that country to be stationed there and to cooperate with Thai armed forces in maintaining the territorial integrity of that country.[5]

2 *Current Notes*, XXXIII, 37.
3 The government on Jan. 25, 1963, announced the grant of an additional £A250,000 for urgently needed supplies for the village-hamlet programs. *Current Notes*, XXXIV, 62.
4 *Current Notes*, XXXIV, 36-37.
5 *Current Notes*, XXXIV, 37.

The increasing Australian involvement in Vietnam followed the American pattern, only on a much smaller scale. On June 8, 1964, Defense Minister Shane Paltridge announced that the Australian government, after consultation with the government of South Vietnam, had decided to increase from thirty to sixty the number of army instructors engaged in training Vietnamese in jungle warfare and village defense, and that consultations were proceeding for the provision of twenty more "specialist instructors and advisers in those fields where they were particularly required by the South Vietnamese." Three new Caribou transport aircraft would shortly be deployed to South Vietnam and another three in a few months.[6] Since 1962, Australia had extended economic aid to South Vietnam to the value of £A3,500,000 for defense support and social and economic development of villages. In early 1965 the number of army instructors was increased from sixty to one hundred.

A further step was taken in April, 1965. On the twenty-ninth of that month, Menzies announced in the House of Representatives that upon request from the government of South Vietnam and after "close consultation" with the government of the United States, his government had decided to provide an infantry battalion (about eight hundred men) for service in South Vietnam. He justified the decision on the grounds of the "gravity of the situation." There was "ample evidence to show that with the support of the North Vietnamese and other Communist powers, the Vietcong has been preparing on a more substantial scale than hitherto insurgency designed to destroy South Vietnamese government control and to disrupt by violence the life of the local people. The rate of infiltration of guerrillas from North Viet Nam has been increasing." He also noted that in recent months the United States had made "historic decisions" to extend increased military assistance to South Vietnam.[7] On August 18

[6] *Current Notes*, XXXV, 49-51.
[7] *Current Notes*, XXXVI, 178-80.

he announced that three hundred fifty additional supporting troops would be sent to South Vietnam.

The decision of the government to send combat troops into Vietnam was criticized sharply by the opposition. Already in July, 1964, a Labor member had questioned the legal basis for the presence in South Vietnam of instructors, advisers, and arms and military equipment from the United States and Australia. Barwick answered that the legal basis for the Australian position rested upon the "invitation" of the government of South Vietnam to Australia to make a "contribution" to their security. On August 13, Menzies stated that the Australian commitment flowed from the "general obligations assumed under SEATO to resist armed attack and to counter subversive activities within the treaty area."[8]

Arthur Calwell made a slashing attack on the decision. In a speech in the House of Representatives on May 4, 1965, he argued that this would promote the interests of China in Asia and the Pacific. The policy meant the substitution of military for economic aid and the support of a reactionary, unpopular, and corrupt regime. It was dangerous because it pushed nationalism toward Communism. Should North Vietnam be reduced, a vacuum would be created into which China undoubtedly would move. Moreover, Calwell argued, political subversion, not military invasion, was the real threat from China. He also charged that by sending a quarter of "our pitifully small, effective military strength to distant Viet Nam, this government dangerously denudes Australia and its immediate environs of effective power." Australia's role should have been to encourage negotiation. "By its decision the Australian government has withdrawn from the ranks of negotiators. We have reduced ourselves to impotence in the field of diplomacy."

"We believe," he concluded, "that America must not be

8 *Current Notes,* XXXV, 29.

humiliated and must not be forced to withdraw. But we are convinced that sooner or later the dispute in Viet Nam must be settled through the councils of the United Nations. If it is necessary to back with a peace force the authority of the United Nations, we would support Australian participation to the hilt. But we believe that the military involvement in the present form decided on by the Australian government represents a threat to Australia's standing in Asia and above all, to the security of this nation."[9]

The Labor members of Parliament were neither united nor consistent in their views on aid to Vietnam. J. F. Cairns, a member of the shadow cabinet, believed that "the reunification of Viet-Nam would not mean more than a marginal change of influences in Laos, Cambodia and Thailand;" that while there would be an increase of Chinese influence in the area, Chinese invasion or occupation of Vietnam was unlikely; that the United States could not win the war; that there must be negotiations to bring it to an end, and that there was no possibility of negotiations unless "the National Liberation Front is near the centre of the negotiating table on the side opposite to the United States."[10] "What we should be requiring is a ceasefire now to negotiate, if what we want is to prevent a greater war."[11] But K. E. Beazley, Labor member for Freemantle, was highly critical of the "philosophy of demanding the 'getting out of' such situations as that of Viet Nam." This philosophy did not go far enough. "If it were carried as far as it should go, of course, it would be a part of an effective world settlement." The situation in Vietnam was part of a global state of tension and its settlement could be achieved only in a global setting, he said. "I am all in favor of the West getting out of Berlin if the Soviet Union gets out of East Germany. . . . There is a very

[9] *CPD*, House, XLVI, 1102-7.
[10] *Living With Asia*, 74-75.
[11] *CPD*, House, XLV, 250, March 23, 1965.

strong case for the United States getting out of Viet Nam, and allowing self-determination there, but there is precisely the same case for the Soviet Union getting out of Hungary and allowing self-determination there."[12]

The difficulties of the Labor party in arriving at a clear, consistent policy on the Vietnam situation are evident from the resolution of the Labor Party Executive of February 18, 1965. The presence of American forces was "necessary and justified as a holding operation," a temporary measure so that the people of Vietnam could in due course be allowed "to decide by their own votes on their own government and to ensure the physical independence of that government," but western support should be withdrawn from "the forces of reaction, oppression and tyranny" in South Vietnam and "a program of full scale economic and social assistance" should be implemented. To whom this assistance should be given after support of the existing government had been withdrawn was not indicated by the resolution. The American escalation of hostilities was condoned: "The case for the American action of recent days, as based on the aim of shortening the war and achieving a negotiated settlement, which would establish and maintain the rights of the South Vietnamese people, deserves sympathetic Australian understanding." The resolution castigated the government for refusal or failure to support the efforts of the prime minister of Canada, the secretary-general of the United Nations, and others who sought a negotiated peace. "Instead, the Australian government appears to prefer to line itself with the mad-headed and extremist elements both in America and in other countries, which are seeking to push their governments to the brink of total war." Australia should seek a Geneva-type conference to work out "a peaceful and enduring solution." Concerning relations with the United States, the resolution

---

[12] *CPD*, House, XLV, 253.

admitted that "the position remains true that cooperation between Australia and America is of crucial importance and must be maintained."[13]

The government obviously was concerned about the likelihood of being charged with having yielded to pressure from the United States. Henry Cabot Lodge was in Canberra only a week before Menzies announced the decision to send combat troops to South Vietnam. Menzies seemed to anticipate such charges, for in his announcement he said, "In case there is any misunderstanding, I think I should say that we decided in principle some time ago—weeks and weeks ago—that we would be willing to do this if we received the necessary request from the government of South Viet Nam and the necessary collaboration with the United States. This is not to be regarded as something that has suddenly arisen out of more recent events." He concluded his announcement with a message from President Johnson expressing Johnson's pleasure at the decision of the Australian government to provide an infantry battalion for service in South Vietnam.

Two aspects of Australian relations with the United States are evident in Menzies' announcement. On the one hand, the government wanted to avoid exposing itself to the charge that it had reduced Australia to a satellite of America, a charge frequently made by Laborites. On the other hand, the government hoped to gain popular approval from evidences of close, harmonious relations with the country to which Australia must look for its ultimate security. At least part of the public viewed it this way. The *Sydney Morning Herald* stated that it was in Australia's continuing interest to remain a valuable ally of the United States: "What claim would we have on American help when our hour of need struck if we stood aside from the United States now? This is

[13] Quoted by T. B. Millar, "Problems of Australian Foreign Policy, Jan. to June, 1965," *Australian Journal of Politics and History*, XI, 271-72.

the crux of the matter in terms of the plainest national self-interest."[14]

The Australian government fully supported the American government's policy in Vietnam, or stated more correctly, its views were identical with those of the United States. In his foreign policy statement to the House on March 23, 1965, Hasluck said: "Australia's own analysis of the situation has brought us to the belief that the United States' action is necessary for the defeat of the aggression against Asian peoples and is also an essential step towards the building in Asia of the conditions of peace and progress. We also believe that in their resistance to China they are preventing an alteration in the world balance of power which would be in favor of the Communists and which would increase the risk of world war." To the charge that the United States and its allies were creating the risk of a wider war he answered that "the alternative would be to allow the systematic mounting of campaigns of guerrilla warfare and terrorism to undermine non-communist governments one after another in South-East Asia."[15]

When the American government began air attacks on targets in North Vietnam, Hasluck made a statement on Feb. 8, 1965, stating that "the method was fitting and the targets were appropriate," and that "it will hearten the free countries of Asia to see this evidence of the continual determination of the United States to assist free peoples to defend their freedom and to maintain their independence. The aggressor holds the answer. He either has to stop or be stopped."[16] In a speech on July 16, 1965, Hasluck said that "we believe that our stake in preserving the degree of stability which has been secured in South-East Asia is as great, or greater, than that of the United States itself. It would not be

[14] May 5, 1965.
[15] *Current Notes*, XXXVI, 119ff. See also his statements to the House on Aug. 18, 1965, *Ibid.*, 455ff., and Oct. 19, 1965, *Ibid.*, 619ff.
[16] *Current Notes*, XXXVI, 99-100.

in the Australian character or consistent with our national self-respect to stand aside while the Americans do the fighting in what we know are our own interests and causes."[17] Menzies expressed this view even more strongly. At a press conference on July 13, 1965, he said, "Now I find that there are some people who say, 'Well, why should Australia be in South Viet Nam?' It would be quite proper I think to answer that by saying 'Well, why is the United States in South Viet Nam?' Her obligations are no greater than ours. In one sense, her interests may be thought to be somewhat less immediate than ours."[18] He was opposed to the neutralization of the region as a solution. "A country that is neutral with more than 600,000,000 Chinese on its flank and its friends thousands of miles away, is not likely to remain neutral very long."[19] In supporting the American position, Sir Robert sometimes took a less flexible stand than President Johnson. Two days before Johnson's Baltimore speech, in which he proposed a billion dollar development program for Southeast Asia and offered to negotiate over Vietnam. Sir Robert declared: "If I am the only prime minister left to denounce it [a negotiated peace], I denounce it."[20]

In justifying sending troops to Vietnam, Menzies at times emphasized the necessity to defend Australia "in depth" and to meet the enemy as far as possible from Australia's shores. For a country which was anxious to establish close relations with Asian countries, this might have an adverse effect, as A. G. Whitlam, deputy leader of the Labor party in Parliament, pointed out. What was good sense and good strategy for the Australians might be regarded by the Asians as a determination by the Australians to fight their wars on Asian soil.[21]

[17] Devonshire, Tasmania, July 16, 1965, *Current Notes*, XXXVI, 424.
[18] *Current Notes*, XXXVI, 415.
[19] Address to the American-Australian Association, June 29, 1964, *Current Notes*, XXXV, 50.
[20] *Sydney Daily Mirror*, April 12, 1965.
[21] *Canberra Times*, March 4, 1965.

The opposition frequently accused the government of not having a foreign policy of its own and of unquestioningly following the lead of America or Britain. A Labor member charged that "the Menzies government . . . is incapable of expressing an Australian view with regard to foreign policy. It has demonstrated this by either giving what might be termed rubber stamp approval to the foreign policies of the United States of America and the United Kingdom or following the more regressive of the two."[22] This sensitive issue again was pressed after the visit to Canberra of United States Vice President Hubert Humphrey in February, 1966. On January 20 Secretary of Defense Robert McNamara had stated before the Congressional Armed Services Committee that the United States desired greater combat aid from Australia, and Humphrey's visit was regarded widely as promoting this objective. At the press conference held by Prime Minister Holt, who succeeded Menzies on January 26, 1966, and Vice President Humphrey on February 19, the two leaders were asked if the United States had requested increased combat forces for service in Vietnam. Humphrey's reply was evasive, but Holt quickly attempted to relieve him of embarrassment. "He has raised no question with us," Holt said, "which implies or presents any pressure of any kind to this country. . . . I can say with entire sincerity and frankness that at no time has any pressure been put upon this country of an improper or irregular character by the government of the United States. But," he added, "we are engaged together in Viet Nam" and the United States had very substantially increased its armed forces in the conflict, and it need be no mystery that under the circumstances there were discussions of what the various countries involved could do.[23] In reply to a question about how far the United States government had taken the Australian government into its confidence, Holt replied that the "Australian gov-

[22] Uren, Sept. 30, 1964, *CPD*, House, XLIV, 1628.
[23] *Current Notes*, XXXVII, 84.

ernment believes that the cooperation, the supply of information and discussion from the United States government could not be closer."[24]

On March 8, 1966, Holt informed Parliament that the government, at the request of the government of South Vietnam, had decided to increase the Australian forces in Vietnam from 1,500 to 4,500 men. The battalion serving there would be replaced by a self-contained task force, including support.[25] This news naturally provoked more debate and questions. Calwell referred to the hostilities in Vietnam as "a jungle war which is unwinnable,"[26] while another Labor member asked the acting minister for external affairs "what say, if any," the Australian government had in the conduct of military operations in Vietnam? The reply was that the Australian forces in Vietnam were under the control of their own commanding officer "who has the facility of communicating with the Australian government, just as was the situation with the Australian forces engaged in various theatres in the last world war."[27]

The same difficulties and dilemmas are reflected in Calwell's speeches. They reflect deep concern about the situation in Vietnam but fail to present a clear and consistent policy toward it. He regarded Vietnam as "the most potentially explosive" situation the world has had to face since World War II, more dangerous than Korea or Cuba. "Possibility of mistakes and the impossibility of controlling and limiting the results of those mistakes are far greater than in either of the two earlier situations. Each day brings new reports full of foreboding." He acknowledges Australia's dependence upon the United States for security. "We want the American presence, strong and powerful, in Asia and the Pacific. We want it because Australia needs it until all

[24] *Current Notes,* XXXVII, 87.
[25] *Current Notes,* XXXVII, 111.
[26] *Current Notes,* XXXVII, 146.
[27] *Current Notes,* XXXVII, 149-50.

nations are prepared to disarm." Moreover, "aggression in
all forms must be resisted." Yet if China became involved
in the hostilities, the war could have no other objective than
the destruction of China. What then is the way out? Negotiation—"negotiation from strength, negotiation now, while
she [the United States] has in Asia, the strength to negotiate."[28]

Opponents of Australian participation in the war in Vietnam frequently charged the government with failure or
inability to state its war aims. Holt, in a statement in Parliament on March 31, 1966, sought to clarify his government's
war aims, and stated that the objectives were (1) to help
the government of South Vietnam, at its request, resist the
armed aggression of Communist North Vietnam; (2) to free
the 15,000,000 people of South Vietnam "from the threat of
oppression and terrorism which would be their lot under the
domination of the Communists of the North and help establish conditions under which they will be able to choose and
develop free from coercion of any kind the forms of government and society, which they themselves want;" (3) "to
leave no one in doubt that we in Australia are prepared and
resolved to honor our treaty commitments and our alliances
and to stand firm with our allies in the face of aggression,
whether direct or indirect;" (4) to insure that the spread of
Communism in Southeast Asia is checked and to give "encouragement to those moderate elements in the various
countries of the region whom we are already supporting in
the work of modernization and economic and social progress;" (5) to seek a peaceful settleemnt of the conflict
through negotiations on the basis of the Geneva Agreement.
"Our basic aims," he said, "are not only clear and limited—
they are sound."

He concluded that "Australia has a vital interest in the

effective presence and active participation of the United States as a great power in the area of Asia and the Pacific. We have an obligation to support the United States in this role—an obligation arising from our treaty relationships, from our role as an ally in supporting the United States in international diplomacy and politics, and from the fact that our international interests are directly involved in preserving South-East Asia from aggression and from Communist domination."[29]

The government was questioned also about the relationship between Australia's actions in Vietnam and Australian membership in SEATO, with the implication that the sending of troops to Vietnam was not covered by that agreement, if not in violation of it. Hasluck sought to give a careful, realistic answer to the question. "It would be wrong to say," he said, "that the Australian government is acting today in Viet Nam solely because it is obliged to do so under SEATO. Even if SEATO did not exist, Australia would want to see Communist aggression deterred and resisted in the region of South and South-East Asia. SEATO helps to deter and resist aggression. SEATO is an agreement and a working practical arrangement in which Australia adheres to and observes in pursuit of our own interests and policies. Our actions in SEATO are in pursuance of our obligations through SEATO but are not because of SEATO alone."

He noted that the obligations under SEATO were separate as well as joint, individual as well as collective. The SEATO Council had made no decision for collective action, but it affirmed in 1964 and reaffirmed in 1965 that "the defeat of

[29] *Current Notes,* XXXVII, 151-52. Hasluck frequently has stated this general position. In a speech in the House of Representatives on March 10, 1966, he said: "Our whole interest as Australians is in the advance of all the peoples of this region to a new and brighter future of freedom, independence and opportunity. What threatens this freedom and independence and what dims their hope for the future is the dread of domination by the new imperialism of China and the throttling grip of Communist aggressors." *Ibid.,* 123-24.

this Communist campaign is essential not only to the security of the Republic of Viet Nam but to that of South-East Asia. . . . Member governments recognized that the state of affairs in Viet Nam . . . constitutes a flagrant challenge to the essential purpose for which they had associated together under the Treaty; to resist aggression." In the absence of a collective decision, each member state had "to decide for itself what action it should take, in the light of its own interests and in the light of its capacities." While South Vietnam was not a member of SEATO, it was a protocol state and thus under its protection.[30]

Hasluck also has given some indication about what he believes the peace objectives should be. After the aggression has been checked, the powers chiefly concerned might return to the 1954 Geneva Agreement as a starting point for attempts "to achieve the security and stability of the region as an essential preliminary to reconstruction for the future. The reality is that we will not reach that starting point again unless and until the Soviet Union and China, as well as the United States, are willing to do so."[31]

MOST NEWSPAPERS SUPPORTED the government's policy in sending combat troops to Vietnam, but their reasons differed. One analyzed the move as help for the United States now so that Australia could expect aid in time of trouble. "Help for the United States now is Australia's main chance of survival in the future."[32] Another paper observed that most Australians desire the physical presence of the United States in Southeast Asia, but some had misgivings about sending combat troops to South Vietnam. "Yet the dilemma is clear: if we want an American military presence we must be prepared

[30] House, May 30, 1966, *Current Notes*, XXXVII, 257-60.
[31] Speech at a Liberal party meeting, July 16, 1965, *Current Notes*, XXXVI, 429.
[32] *Sydney Sunday Telegraph*, May 23, 1965.

to join with it; if we don't, we must be prepared to live with the alternative."[33] Still another metropolitan daily, sharply criticizing Calwell's position, asserted that most of his premises were wrong. It observed that "if all Viet Nam were to pass under Communist rule, inevitably Chinese influence would be thrust so much further south."[34] A Tasmanian paper said that Calwell virtually denied Australia's commitment under SEATO.[35]

A daily in the largest city in the country with a large circulation supported the government's policy without reservation, chiefly on two grounds: (1) that it was in Australia's continuing interest to remain a valued ally of the United States and (2) Australia had an interest in the defense of South Vietnam. "The outcome of the war in Vietnam will affect Australia far more diligently and immediately than the United States and it is therefore logical and proper that Australia should play as full a part as it can in ensuring that the war is not lost and the last practical defence against Communist expansion reached."[36] In commenting upon the American peace effort, this paper said: "It seems that blinkered rulers of Hanoi and Peking, largely insulated from the world, wrapped in their dogma, confident of their strength, have convinced themselves that they only need to stand firm and American resolution will falter and fail. When dealing with minds so rigid the very intensity of the American drive for peace may defeat its object, because it is all too likely to be interpreted as weakness."[37]

While nearly all the great journals of the country believed the government's Vietnam policy was justified,[38] some were unhappy about the secondary role which Australia, under

[33] *Canberra Times*, June 9, 1965.
[34] *Adelaide Advertiser*, May 6, 1965.
[35] *Hobart Mercury*, May 5, 1965.
[36] *Sydney Morning Herald*, May 5, 1965.
[37] *Sydney Morning Herald*, Dec. 31, 1965. See also editorial, May 5, 1965.
[38] In addition to above, see editorials in the *Brisbane Courier-Mail*, June 11, 1964; *Melbourne Herald*, May 24, 1965.

the circumstances, necessarily played. "While it is obviously right for us to support the American appeal for aid," the *Melbourne Age* said, "it would add strength to our support if the aid were clearly provided in pursuit of an Australian policy in Viet Nam. Demands are being made on Australian military aid today in an increasing range of situations, in none of which is Australian policy a prime or determining factor. This may be the price of alliances. It could be, however, a stimulus to the creation of essentially Australian policies.[39] Some papers were concerned about the potentially dangerous scattering of the country's meager military resources.[40]

One influential newspaper, *The Australian,* was actually hostile toward the government's policy in Vietnam. It called the decision to send combat troops "reckless." Australian soldiers were being sent "into a savage, revolutionary war in which the Americans are grievously involved—so that America may shelve a tiny part of her embarrassment." The decision was wrong, no matter how it was viewed, the paper said. Australia's contingent could have no significant value and would be only a political pawn "in a situation for which Australia has no responsibility whatever. . . . It is wrong because it deliberately and coldly runs counter to the mounting wave of international anxiety about the shape of the Viet Nam war and justification and perils of America's military escalation. . . . Australia has lined up her generations against the hatred and contempt of resurgent Asian peoples —without adding one iota of confidence or strength to the tragically embroiled American nation. It could be that our historians will recall this day with tears."[41]

The Australian reflected an isolationist point of view.

[39] May 11, 1964.
[40] *Canberra Times,* May 5, 1965; *Melbourne Age,* Aug. 19, 1965.
[41] April 30, 1965. A variant of this critical attitude was that of the *Sydney Daily Mirror,* which echoed Calwell's views that western policy in Vietnam

Australia had achieved "an unusual and advantageous position" in its "geographical semi-isolation," which should be exploited "in asserting our exceptional independence before the eyes of the Afro-Asian nations where, whether we like it or not—and we must get to like it—our long term political interests lie."[42] It suggested that there was cause for fear that the United States, "shaken by a debacle in South Viet Nam, may think that a withdrawal to fortress America may be the best policy for the Pacific. All the more reason for Australia to be active in seeking a solution in Viet Nam which would be a guaranteed compromise."[43]

The government was criticized by some sections of the Christian churches. A number of Anglican bishops wrote to Menzies expressing deep concern that "our government should be seen to be taking positive steps, with others, towards an honorable and peaceful settlement of the fighting in Viet Nam." Sir Robert replied that certain conditions were necessary before there could be successful negotiations, namely: (1) the other parties should be willing to negotiate; (2) there should be a genuine cease-fire, strictly and honorably observed; and (3) there should be some reasonable assurance that aggression and subversion will come to an end. None of these conditions were present, he said.

The bishops came back with a letter charging the South Vietnam government with two serious breaches of the spirit and the letter of the Geneva Agreements, "with full knowledge and approval, and active support of the United States," the continued refusal to hold free elections and the grant of military bases to a foreign power. They repeated their hope that Menzies would use his "great influence to support

---

had failed, that negotiations were inevitable and should begin at once. "It is surely up to Australia, as a Pacific power, to try to initiate a move for a cease-fire as a first step towards a negotiated peace." March 24, 1965.

[42] May 20, 1965.

[43] March 12, 1965. How and by whom the compromise, if it could be reached, would be guaranteed, the editorial did not indicate.

the possibility of negotiations. We cannot think that we, or others more distinguished, are hopelessly deluded in asking that negotiations become the declared objective of Australian policy." Sir Robert replied that since the Communist government of North Vietnam would not permit free elections, it was unreasonable to expect South Vietnam to proceed with elections, because it could only result in turning the South over to the Communists. As for bases, the government of South Vietnam had not granted military bases to the United States; it had called upon America for help to repel aggression. He and his colleagues, he said, "are constantly aware of our duties to our country and our people. One of these duties is to do what we can to keep the peace, and to help others to keep it. Another is to be acutely aware of the need to preserve the security of Australia. It would be a sorry day, if by undermining the will and capacity to resist in South-East Asia, we found aggressive Communism moving nearer to our own shores. We will observe our obligations under SEATO and ANZUS not only because Australia has pledged its word—a reason compelling enough, in all conscience—but because those obligations have to be accepted on behalf of our own free future."[44]

Opposition to conscription was voiced by semi-official Catholic newspapers. *The Advocate,* published in Melbourne, wrote that the government had no mandate to send conscripts to Vietnam, since war had not been declared. "Conscription is in itself an evil thing, justified only in an emergency"; without this necessity it is "a violation of a basic human freedom."[45] The *Catholic Worker* questioned whether it was morally right for the voters, who had not

---

[44] The letters of the bishops are dated March 12 and April 9, 1965; those of the prime minister, March 24 and April 20. See *Current Notes,* XXXVI, 139ff., 182ff.

[45] Quoted from *The Advocate* by the Canberra Correspondent in the *Straits' Times,* March 24, 1966.

volunteered themselves, to compel the voteless young men to fight for them.[46]

PROBABLY ONE REASON that Menzies resigned as prime minister in January, 1966, was that near the end of the year an arduous election campaign was coming up. His retirement in favor of a younger man in a sense was the beginning of the political campaign, and it became obvious very early that the Labor party would make the government's Vietnam policy a major issue. Also, it soon became clear that the departure of Sir Robert from the ministry did not mean a change in the government's foreign policy, or that the Holt ministry would evade or soft-pedal the Vietnam issue.

Holt went to Vietnam in March and to Washington and London in June and July. In Washington he endorsed President Johnson's decision to step up the bombing of North Vietnam, calling it a "military necessity" for the security of the whole region. The defense effort in Vietnam already had resulted in "the strengthening of all South-East Asia."[47] In their joint communique the two leaders expressed their "determination" to repel aggression against South Vietnam and their "full confidence" that their efforts would be successful.[48] In both Washington and London, Holt criticized some Western European countries for turning their backs upon Asia, since their economies had been restored by Marshall Plan aid. He specifically exempted Britain from that criticism, because it had borne the brunt of the defense of Malaysia. Obviously he was speaking chiefly of France.[49]

[46] Quoted in Australian newsletter by Richard Cloake in Sydney, *South China Morning Post* (Hong Kong), April 30, 1966.
[47] *The New York Times*, July 6, 1966.
[48] *The New York Times*, July 15, 1966. Holt visited Washington twice—on his way to London and on his way back—and had conferences with President Johnson both times.
[49] Holt not only defended American bombing of North Vietnam, but in

The Holt government clearly was prepared to make its complete commitment to the defense of South Vietnam the chief issue in the election campaign. Its leaders were convinced that it was in Australia's interest to be in Vietnam. They were not uncritical followers of the United States; they did not support the United States in the hope of American military aid in the future, but from the conviction that if the peace of the world was being threatened anywhere, it was in Southeast Asia. Hasluck emphasized this view, and in August, when the campaign was beginning to intensify, he told Parliament that the United States is supporting international security in a region where "our own danger is immeasurably greater than any danger to America, where the stake in peace is more fateful to us than for them."[50] The government's earnestness about its commitment in Vietnam was evident from the announcement by the federal treasurer that the defense expenditures in the new budget would be increased $282.3 million to a total of $1.1 billion.[51]

In May, the Labor party leadership issued a manifesto promising that if it won the election, it would without delay withdraw all conscripts serving in Vietnam and the remaining troops "as soon as practicable and in consultation with the United States." Evidences of disunity developed, however. In a surprising speech in Parliament in August, a Labor member strongly defended Australian military participation in Vietnam and then resigned from the party. His views were somewhat crass. "No member of this House," he said, "can afford to throw away the insurance policy we have with

London he personally rebuked Prime Minister Wilson for dissociating the United Kingdom from the bombing of Haiphong. When a member of the British Parliament raised a question about this dissociation, Wilson replied: "It is well known that, on the question of having troops in Vietnam and the question of the bombing of Hanoi and Haiphong, the government of Australia and ourselves take different positions. We are both sovereign and independent countries and are entitled to do so, for what would appear to be good reasons in both cases." *The Times* (London), July 13, 1966.

[50] *The New York Times*, Aug. 19, 1966.
[51] *The New York Times*, Aug. 17, 1966.

America. The premiums must be paid. Paid gladly. Australia has always honored its obligations."[52] Despite the growing disunity on the issue Calwell refused to soften his views. He called the hostilities in Vietnam "a wicked, senseless, unwinnable war . . . a war which has no moral or legal justification" and promised Australian withdrawal if his party won the election. However, there was evidence of disagreement on the part of his deputy, Edward Gough Whitlam, who seemed to advocate the withdrawal of conscripts only.[53]

One unusual event marked the election campaign. In mid-October, President and Mrs. Johnson visited Australia, and he was the first American president to visit the country. This expression of friendship and of appreciation for Australia's support in Vietnam was hailed with delight by the government parties.[54] The visit also indicated the importance to President Johnson of the election in Australia.

In the elections, which were held on November 26, the government coalition parties won a resounding victory, increasing their majority in the House of Representatives (124 members) from nineteen to forty-one.

[52] J. S. Benson from Victoria. *The New York Times,* Aug. 28, 1966.
[53] *The New York Times,* Oct. 30, 1966.
[54] An elated Liberal party tactician, when the presidential visit was announced, said, "short of calling on the Almighty, Harold couldn't have hauled in a better ally." See the interesting article "Australia's Harold Holt is the Man on Top Down Under," by Harry Gordon, assistant editor of the *Melbourne Sun,* in *The New York Times Magazine,* Oct. 23, 1966. President Johnson also visited New Zealand where a campaign was likewise in progress. In the election held in New Zealand at the same time, support of the United States in Vietnam likewise was the chief issue. The government won, but not so decisively as in Australia.

7 *An Emerging Policy*

One of the main problems governing security in Asia derives from the lack of balance in the region. . . . There is a natural desire in the countries of the region, as part of the winning of independence and national sovereignty, to look upon defence and security as primarily a matter of their own concern. Those countries in the region which enter into treaty relationships with external powers do so realistically but in an awareness that they are subject to criticism from opposition elements within their own communities and from abroad. The fact is, however, in this region that a self-supporting security system is not at this time practicable. . . . This, of course, entails the presence in the region of foreign troops and bases, with all the constantly recurring political and diplomatic problems to which this gives rise. But it is important that our Asian neighbors appreciate this necessity and neither seek to weaken the security of the region, nor seek to distort the balance as between themselves by working towards an early removal of these bases.

SIR GARFIELD BARWICK
Minister for External Affairs
Before Australian Institute
of Political Science
Jan. 25, 1964.

THERE ARE A few obvious influences in Australia's defense problem. First of all, Australia is a "white island in a brown sea." A historical, political, and cultural outpost of Western Europe, this smallest continent lies anchored off the insular appendages of Asia at a great distance from England and the United States, its closest associates. An Australian scholar has noted that "the central problem of Australia's foreign policy is how to reconcile our geography with our history."[1]

Secondly, though the country is developing rapidly, its population is small. At best, Australia is a middle or an intermediate power. Also, its small population—less than 12,000,000—is spread over nearly 3,000,000 square miles.

All of its great cities, located on an enormously extenuated coastline, are vulnerable to attack. Between crowded Asia and sparsely populated Australia lie numerous islands which can provide bases for attack on it. The geographic isolation of the country detracts from its value in world strategy, though its rapid industrialization and cultural development give it a growing importance in world politics.

As was noted in the introductory chapter, Australia had no foreign policy of its own until World War II, or, more specifically, until the fall of Singapore in February, 1942. The same is true of defense policy. Australians were opposed to maintaining large armed forces in peacetime, probably because they felt little need for them since Australia was not in imminent danger of attack. In both World Wars, when England was in difficulty, Australians efficiently equipped and supported large expeditionary forces. Thus, when Japan struck at Pearl Harbor and then moved into Southeast Asia, Australia's military forces were in the Middle East and Malaya, and the homeland was practically defenseless.

In this sudden, very threatening situation the people of

[1] W. Macmahon Ball in *Taking Stock: Aspects of Mid-Century Life in Australia*, ed. W. V. Aughterson (Melbourne, 1953), 35.

Australia understandably were alarmed. Prime Minister John Curtin expressed near-panic in an article in the *Melbourne Herald,* in which he declared that he refused to accept "the dictum that the Pacific struggle must be treated as a subordinate segment of the general conflict," that "without any inhibitions of any kind, I make it quite clear that Australia looks to America, free of any pangs as to our traditional links with the United Kingdom."[2]

Under the circumstances it was not surprising that an atmosphere of acrimony and recrimination between the Australian and British governments should develop. British Prime Minister Winston Churchill was critical of Curtin's "outpourings of anxiety . . . which was flaunted around the world by our enemies." He also thought it "remarkable that in this deadly crisis . . . they did not join together in a common effort. But such was their party phlegm and rigidity that local politics ruled unshaken. The Labour Party, with its majority of two, monopolized the whole executive power, and conscription even for home defence was banned."[3] Nor could he "forbear a reference to the strong support which Australian parties, particularly the Labour Party, had given before the war both to the neglect of our defences and to the policy of appeasement."[4]

WHY AUSTRALIANS REGARDED the fall of Singapore as an unmitigated calamity is revealed in the strained notes of Curtin to Churchill in the dark days of the Japanese invasion of Malaya. In a telegram on January 18, 1942, Curtin reminded Churchill that as early as 1933, when the Committee of Imperial Defence was considering the protection of Singapore,

---

[2] Winston Churchill, *The Second World War,* 4 vols. (Boston, 1950), IV, 8.
[3] Churchill, IV, 4, 5, 8.
[4] Churchill, IV, 15.

the high commissioner for Australia had noted the "grave effects that would flow from the loss of Singapore or the denial of its use to the main fleet," that "in the last resort, the whole internal defence system of Australia was based on the integrity of Singapore and the presence of a capital fleet there," and if that was not a "reasonable possibility, Australia, in balancing a doubtful naval security against invasion, would have to provide for greater land and air forces as a deterrent against such risk." The United Kingdom government in 1937 gave assurances of its purpose to make Singapore impregnable. Australians were brought up to believe in this "conception of the Empire and local defence." It was trust in this conception which had influenced Australia to cooperate in other theaters of war, in spite of its relatively small resources in relation to its needs for national defense in case of a Pacific war.[5]

Defense policy was debated in the 1930's. The government favored concentrating primarily upon the army, envisaging cooperation with Great Britain and the Empire by an expeditionary force. Australia trusted British sea power, with its supporting bases at Aden, Ceylon, Singapore, and Hong Kong. Moreover, with western powers controlling the countries between Australia and China and Japan, which represented the only potential threats to the nation, and with three friendly powers having strong defensive positions in the region, a threat to Australia's security seemed remote. The Labor party, on the other hand, advocated the defense of Australia as the primary objective and to this end advocated the development of the air force and the navy. The 1937 election campaign centered around this issue, and the government won decisively. Though the government policy was based upon Singapore as a bastion of defense in the region, Australia did not contribute to the cost of the base.

[5] Churchill, IV, 14.

EVEN BEFORE WORLD WAR II, Australians began to think in terms of a Pacific pact as a solution to their security problem. Prime Minister J. A. Lyons, at the Imperial Conference of 1937, proposed such an agreement, and Evatt, as foreign minister, talked much about regional associations. He seemed to have two types in mind: one to promote economic development and social welfare in the countries of the region, and a second to insure security. In 1947 he argued in the House of Representatives that "we must work for a harmonious association of democratic states in the South-East Asia area, and see in the development of their political maturity opportunity for greatly increased political, cultural and commercial cooperation."[6] The establishment of the South Pacific Commission in 1947 in some degree met the first purposes; the creation of a regional security arrangement is a longer, more complex story.

An account of the Australian-New Zealand agreement, the first of Australia's regional pacts, already has been given.[7] It called for "a regional zone of defence" within the "framework of a general system of world security" (Article 13). Pending the "reestablishment of law and order and the inauguration of a system of general security," the two governments "agreed that it would be proper" for them "to assume full responsibility for policing or sharing in policing such areas in the Southwest and South Pacific as may from time to time be agreed upon" (Article 15). Evatt likely had two objectives; first, to provide for the future security of his country and, secondly, to see that Australia assumed the role which Great Britain had been playing in the region. "What we are claiming," he said, "is that we must have a primary and principal responsibility in determining the future of the

[6] Feb. 6, 1947, *Commonwealth Parliamentary Debates*, House, CXC, 164.
[7] See Chapter 2.

particular region in which we live. No Australian government worth the name should fail to make this claim."[8] The question of a regional security agreement was also involved in the dispute about Manus Island. Evatt by his maneuvers hoped to obtain from the United States a commitment to defend the Southwest Pacific.[9]

THE NORTH ATLANTIC TREATY ORGANIZATION had been established not long before the Liberal-Country coalition under Menzies came to power. This defense agreement made Australians hope that a similar pact could be concluded for the Southwest Pacific. Percy Spender, the new minister for external affairs, discussed this matter extensively in his foreign policy address to the House of Representatives a few months after he took office.[10] To draw the teeth of Communist imperialism, he proposed a program of "carefully applied measures of economic assistance," but these essentially were long-term measures, and events in Asia could move too quickly for them to take effect. It was, therefore, desirable that all governments "directly interested in the preservation of peace throughout South and South-East Asia and in the advancement of human welfare under the democratic system should consider immediately whether some form of regional pact for common defence is a practical possibility." A purely defensive pact, he felt, was not enough. "We look toward a pact that has also positive aims—the promotion of democratic institutions, higher living standards, increased cultural and commercial ties. . . . The Government regards this as an urgent objective of policy in the fast-moving events of South-East Asia today."

Spender regarded "Communist imperialism" as the threat

[8] *Foreign Policy of Australia: Speeches* (Sydney and London, 1945), 176.
[9] See Chapter 2.
[10] March 9, 1950, *Current Notes*, XXI, 163-64.

to the security of the region, but most Australians at the time were more concerned about the dangers of a rearmed Japan. Anti-Japanese feeling was deep and widespread among Australians, especially among the returned soldiers, many of whom had suffered grievously at the hands of the Japanese as prisoners-of-war. Australia was not pleased with all the terms of the treaty which John Foster Dulles had negotiated for the United States, and the differences in the points of view were revealed in the joint communique issued at the close of Dulles' visit to Canberra to confer with the Australian and New Zealand representatives about the treaty. While there were some differences of approach and emphasis, the three representatives agreed, said the statement, it was "essential not to leave a power vacuum in Japan which could easily be filled by unfriendly forces," but also that a "resurgence of the old Japanese militarism would be a disaster. . . . Ways and means of avoiding such possible developments were considered." Significantly, the communique stated that "no proposals of any character to rearm Japan were considered." The Australian and New Zealand representatives stressed the importance of security arrangements. "These points of view received the sympathetic consideration of the representative of the United States."[11]

Thus, the stage was set for the ANZUS treaty. External Affairs Minister Casey—though he quoted with approval part of the report by the United States Senate Foreign Relations Committee that Australia and New Zealand could agree to a generous treaty imposing no restrictions upon Japanese rearmament only if the United States would formally express concern for their security and agree to stand with them in the event of an attack—nevertheless said that "it is incorrect to describe the treaty as a guarantee by the United States, exacted by us as a condition for entering into the Japanese Treaty." Australian government spokesmen identified Com-

11 Feb. 18, 1951. *Current Notes*, XXII, 106.

munist imperialism as the immediate menace in the region well before the ANZUS treaty was negotiated. Casey said, "Australia's interests and objectives are related to the building of security in the Pacific area generally,"[12] and he pointed out that while Australia was not obliged to do so under the ANZUS treaty, it had committed armed forces on a significant scale in Korea.

While nearly all Australians were agreed on the desirability and even the necessity for a security agreement with the United States and the development of special relations with it, the exclusion of the United Kingdom from ANZUS caused considerable distress. The United States, however, was insistent on limiting the parties to the three countries, probably because it wanted to keep certain countries out, which might have been difficult if the United Kingdom were included. While the Australian government regretted this, it handled the situation well. It argued that the exclusion was only formal, that relations between the United States and the United Kingdom were such that Britain would participate in any important decisions on Asian and Pacific matters. Moreover, it was not necessary, nor possible, for all members of the Commonwealth to be members of the same regional defense alliances. Australia and New Zealand were not members of NATO.[13]

The men chiefly responsible for Australian foreign policy at the time—Menzies, Casey, and Spender—were all known for their great loyalty to Britain, and there was no problem. As Menzies said, "the closest concert between the United States and the British Commonwealth is vital to the common defence . . . [and] . . . to the existence of the free world," as well as essential to Australia's security. "And since in a hundred ways the character of life in the United States so closely resembles that in British communities, it would be strange

12 *Friends and Neighbors: Australia and the World*, 73-74.
13 See Greenwood and Harper, *Australia in World Affairs, 1950-1955* (Melbourne, 1957), 70ff.

indeed if we, the British people, regarded the citizens of the United States as being in a true sense foreigners. When we turn from the world scene to consider our own position in this corner of the world, it would be hard to find any Australian of this generation who did not recognize that the friendship and cooperation of the United States are vital to our own safety. In effect, our natural friendship and intuitive understanding coincide with our legitimate self-interest."[14]

An important question for Australia was the area of application of the treaty. Article 4 speaks of "an armed attack in the Pacific area on any of the Parties," which in Article 5 is further defined "to include an armed attack on the metropolitan territory of any of the Parties, or on the island territories under its jurisdiction in the Pacific or on its armed forces, public vessels or aircraft in the Pacific." This language would seem to be comprehensive enough to cover nearly every situation; Australians have, nevertheless, been concerned about its extent. At the time of the Malaysian confrontation the question was raised in Parliament whether it covered Australian troops facing Indonesians in Borneo. In August, 1965, a Laborite in Parliament asked Hasluck whether the treaty applied only to the Pacific Ocean area or also to other areas where Australian servicemen might be engaged. Hasluck replied that the treaty used the term "Pacific," and its meaning had never been defined, "but all discussions in meetings of the ANZUS council and exchanges with the United States have given the Australian government the confident expectation that the broadest and most liberal interpretation will be given to that term." Under a strict view Western Australia is not in the Pacific area, but he could give the House "my confident assurance that Western Australia certainly would be regarded as one of the regions coming within the ambit of the ANZUS Treaty. Recogniz-

[14] *Current Notes*, XXVI, 285.

ing that the measures we have taken on the defence aspect might put us into a situation invoking the obligations of the ANZUS Treaty, we have taken care to inform the United States in advance of those measures so that it will be well aware of our view of the obligations I have mentioned."[15]

An important obligation is assumed under Article 2 of the treaty. The parties agree "separately and jointly by means of continuous and effective self-help and mutual aid" to "maintain and develop their individual and collective capacity to resist armed attack." Menzies realized the significance of the commitment at the time. "After the treaty has come into effect," he said, "our Australian defence preparations are not merely our own business; we owe them also to our friends without whose help we cannot hope to maintain our freedom against a major challenge."[16]

Despite this commitment Australia did not at once adopt a policy of strong national defense in peacetime, but let its defense forces decline. Australians justified this neglect by the argument that their country could best serve the cause of security in the Pacific by a rapid development of its economy and that heavy defense expenditures would retard economic development. The argument, plausible and pleasant, attracted other adherents than Laborites, who emphasized national development and minimized defense expenditures.

Shocked by the rapid Indonesian military buildup, the Australian government shifted its policy sharply in 1964. On November 10, Menzies announced plans for a large increase in defense spending and for selective compulsory military service. For the first time in Australian history, draftees would be liable to overseas service at any time. The army would be increased from 22,750 to 37,500 men and defense expenditures from £A260 million in 1963-1964 to £A429

[15] *Current Notes*, XXXVI, 513.
[16] "The Pacific Settlement Seen from Australia," *Foreign Affairs*, XXX, 188-96.

million in 1967-1968. In 1966 the government announced a
further increase in defense expenditures to £A550 million.[17]
Labor, which had consistently criticized the government's
defense policies, resumed its traditional hostility to conscription for compulsory military service outside of Australia.

The new defense policy and Australia's support of the
United States in Vietnam became a clear issue in the parliamentary election of November, 1966. The government
coalition won an overwhelming victory.

A significant development in Australian-United States
relations is the establishment of the American naval communications base in the northwestern area of Australia. The
United States erected a huge radio station to serve Polaris
submarines and other naval units in the Indian Ocean and
the regions north of Australia. This installation, in effect,
brings Australia under the American nuclear shield. The
Labor opposition, while welcoming this development that
made Australia an integral part of the American defense
system, opposed the Northwest Cape Base Agreement because it did not provide for joint control, and advocated
renegotiation. Moreover, Labor wanted an agreement that
made the southern hemisphere a nuclear-free zone. Barwick
attacked these proposals as unrealistic, because the American
officials had stated clearly to him that they would not agree
to joint control of the base. If Australia insisted upon joint
control, the United States would not enter into the agreement to build the base. As to the proposed nuclear-free zone,
the American authorities were opposed to it and said that if
it were demanded, the U.S. would "have to rethink its relationship with us in ANZUS."[18] Menzies pointed out that if

---

[17] Holt said on Oct. 31, 1966, that Australian defense expenditures were
then running at one billion Australian dollars annually. The total strength
of the Regular Forces had been increased to 68,500 and by mid-1967 would
be about 80,000, with another 42,000 men in the Citizen Forces and
Reserves. To editor-in-chief, *Straits Times* (Singapore). *Current Notes*,
XXXVII, 675ff.
[18] Oct. 30, 1963, *CPD*, House, XL, 2456-57.

there were an agreement banning nuclear weapons in the region south of the equator, Australia's SEATO and ANZUS allies "could not, except against Australia's will, use nuclear weapons in defence of the region, including Australia, even though Powers north of the Equator used them. Such a policy the government regarded as suicidal."[19] These issues were involved in the 1963 parliamentary elections that the government coalition won.

AUSTRALIA WELCOMED THE Southeast Asia Collective Defense Treaty, though the pact fell short of its desires. Even before the Manila Conference, Menzies announced that his government would accept military commitments in the regional pact proposed by the United States. He had little confidence in the cease-fire in Vietnam and feared that the Communist frontier might reach the southern shores of Indochina.[20] For several years the Australian government had pressed for the enlargement of ANZUS by the inclusion of other countries, both Asian and European, in its membership.

The chief controversy at the conference that drafted the treaty was about the scope of the military provisions. The United States wanted it directed solely against Communism, apparently for two reasons. Asians were extremely sensitive to the issues of imperialism and colonialism, and the United States did not want to make itself vulnerable to that charge. Secondly, it wished to avoid involvement in the India-Pakistan dispute over Kashmir. Australia believed strongly that the treaty should apply to aggression, regardless of its source, and this was supported by a majority of the other delegations. For one thing, Australia feared that restricting the treaty to Communist aggression would repel several Asian states whose membership was highly desirable. Australia's fears were justified. Yielding to their neutralist sentiments,

[19] Oct. 30, 1963, *CPD*, House, XL, 2458.
[20] Aug. 5, 1954, *CPD*, House, V, 63-69.

India and Indonesia responded very negatively to the treaty. Also, Australia naturally desired as wide a protection as possible against aggression in Southeast Asia. The issue was resolved by a compromise; all reference to Communist aggression was deleted from the treaty, but the United States was permitted to attach an "understanding" that its obligations relating to aggression and armed attack "apply only to Communist aggression;" in the event of "other aggression or armed attack" it would consult under the provisions of Article 4. Australia was not happy about this compromise, because it reduced the scope of the American commitment as compared to that of the other signatories, but it was pleased with the general effect of the treaty—the extension to Southeast Asia of the United States' military power.[21]

The SEATO pact represented some gains for Australia. It extended the American commitment beyond that assumed under ANZUS, and it brought the United Kingdom into the treaty, thus forming a bridge with ANZUS. Anglo-American cooperation and alignment in Asia was of the greatest importance to Australians. But Britain, for its limited capability, was too heavily committed in other areas, where its interests were greater, to provide substantial military forces for the defense of Southeast Asia. The treaty lacked teeth; concrete measures for military collaboration were not established. The United States refused to go beyond a plan of mobile defense. Clearly, SEATO was no NATO.[22]

Australians were worried about the defense gap between Singapore and Manila and the difference in strategic priorities between Washington and Canberra. For the United States rim of Asia came first, then the islands from Japan

[21] Australia has, in effect, also reduced its commitment under the treaty by an unwritten rider which excludes its application to inter-Commonwealth relations. See Greenwood and Harper, *Australia in World Affairs, 1956-1960*, 180ff.

[22] For a good analysis of SEATO from the Australian point of view see "Australia and SEATO," by George Modelski in *International Organization*, XIV, 429-37.

to the Philippines, and last Australia and New Zealand, while for Australia the homeland came first, and the islands to the north, and especially Singapore, a close second. This remains a gnawing worry for many Australians, even Laborites. After criticizing the government for believing that "the alliance demands that the weaker partner . . . should follow the line of the most powerful partner, the United States, in all circumstances and irrespective of whether or not Australia considers that line to be right or wrong" a Labor member of Parliament said, "What price would not any of us pay for a situation in which Americans generally said automatically that Australia, like the Philippines, was one of the countries in this area of the world on whose behalf they were prepared to risk a major war?"[23]

An uneven partnership like this may be trying for the weaker member, even with mutual good will. Within the country there is always the possiiblity that the opposition, for political advantage, will criticize the dependent relationship. On the other hand, many Australians frankly believed that since Australia is so dependent upon the United States for security, it should support completely American policy in Asia and thus insure American protection. As a leading newspaper stated: "Australia's primary defence concern is to preserve—and deserve—the assurance of American protection under the ANZUS alliance."[24] One can imagine many Australians saying the same thing in more cynical, less elegant language. Yet in the situation in which the United States finds itself in Vietnam, Australian support has been tremendously important, and the relationship has not been so one-sided. Australians undoubtedly welcomed President Johnson's expression of gratitude during his visit to Australia in October, 1966, when, in effect, he declared that since Australia was giving full support to the United States in Vietnam, the United States would give full support to Aus-

23 Galvin, Oct. 21, 1965, *CPD,* House, XLV, 2098.
24 *Sydney Morning Herald,* Jan. 27, 1966.

tralia. This assurance may have had a marked influence in the election, which the leader of the Labor party deliberately chose to turn into a referendum—an evaluation of Australian international ties—and its party suffered a crushing defeat. "The alliance," an Australian journalist states, "strong and healthy enough before, cannot fail to be strengthened, and the ties between Australia and the United States drawn closer. Self-interest is uppermost in current Australian attitudes; but that is, after all, the firmest base for any alliance."[25]

With their strong social consciousness, Australians are as aware as any people that the advance of Communism by infiltration and subversion cannot be stopped by military measures alone. Australia saw the need for economic aid and technical assistance to the newly independent countries and early made foreign aid a national policy. Though Australia is not yet a highly developed, industrialized country, only the United States, France, and Britain give more on a per capita basis than Australia for foreign economic assistance. Australia has given substantial aid to the countries of Southeast Asia, and that has been in the form of grants, not loans. Australia has subscribed $85 million of the capital of the Asian Development Bank. (The United States and Japan subscribed $200 million of the total capital.) It was insistent that SEATO emphasize economic and social activities. Much was done to win the friendship of Asian neighbors, especially during the decade when Casey was head of the Department of External Affairs.

While from the Australian point of view SEATO left much to be desired, Australian leaders repeatedly have hailed its achievements and reaffirmed their government's solid support. Barwick noted in Parliament in April, 1964, that during the decade of the existence of the Manila Treaty none of the signatories had been the object of Communist aggression

[25] Denis Warner, "Australia Votes to Stay in Vietnam," *The Reporter*, XXXV, 29ff.

"and none of the countries within its protocol, or for that matter within South-East Asia, has been subverted to Communist domination, even though as yet we may not have found the ideal method for repelling subversion and terrorism and making them too costly for their designers."[26]

Holt has testified in much the same vein: "SEATO has its critics, and, of course its imperfections. But the fact is that since its formation, it has held Communism at bay. . . . But, while we have strengthened the foundations of our security, the need for SEATO remains as strong as ever. No region today contains greater dangers for world peace and security than Asia. South-East Asia has been singled out by the Communists as a critical area of challenge. They believe that, if their technique of so-called wars of national liberation can succeed in South Viet Nam, it can be employed with similar success in many other countries."[27]

THE IMPORTANCE OF Singapore in Australian security considerations has been noted frequently. For this reason the declining interests of Britain in Asia since World War II caused concern in Australia. The independence of India, Burma, Ceylon, and finally Malaya all signified diminishing British interests and commitments in South Asia. When Britain withdraws from Aden in 1968, it no longer will have any politically secure bases in the Middle East, East Africa, or Asia. Politically insecure bases consume more security than they produce. As the Singapore base increased in strategic importance, its political security was declining. When

---

[26] *Current Notes*, XXXVII, 37.

[27] At the opening of the eleventh Council Meeting of SEATO at Canberra, June 27, 1966. *Current Notes*, XXXVII, 349. Hasluck at the same meeting said, "In Australia, we place great store upon SEATO. It has been successful in deterring aggression and in encouraging cooperation among like-minded countries. SEATO has value in fields other than military. Through its work in the civil field, SEATO has made, and is making, very useful contributions to the improvement of the lives of the people of its Asian members." *Ibid.*, 368.

Singapore joined Malaysia, the problem of the security of the British base on the island seemed to be solved, but the expulsion of Singapore from the federation again made it politically insecure. While the present government of Singapore does not intend to ask Britain to quit her base on the island, a shift in government regimes could quickly change this policy. Sukarno pressured Singapore to close the British base, offering in return the restoration of normal trade relations with Indonesia. Closing the base, however, would cause unemployment. Moreover, the Singapore government could not ignore the repressive policies of Indonesia against the Chinese in that country.

While Malaya, when it became independent, entered into a defense agreement with Britain (ANZAM), it did not join SEATO, which complicates the security problem of the area. Malaya continued to welcome British and Commonwealth armed forces within its territory, including Australian contingents, but it insisted that these troops confine their operations to Commonwealth territories within the area.

When, because of financial and balance-of-payments problems, word went out from London in 1965 that the United Kingdom would have to reduce its defense expenditures and would have to reconsider its commitments east of Suez, Australians naturally were alarmed. The problem caused them some embarrassment, since annual per capita income in Australia was higher than in Britain, but per capita expenditures for defense were much lower. The United Kingdom was spending 7 percent of its national product on defense and Australia less than 3 percent. This would still be no more than 4 percent after Australia's new armament plans became effective in 1969-1970. The rough, overall cost of the British military presence in Southeast Asia was £300 million a year. A white paper on defense issued by the British government in February, 1966, was rather reassuring and stated, "It is in the Far East and Southern Asia that the greatest danger to peace may lie in the next decade, and some of our partners in the Commonwealth may be directly threatened. We believe that it is right that Britain should continue to maintain a military presence in this area."[28]

The days of cheap defense for Australia obviously were over.[29] While Britain was insistent that it would have to reduce expenditures in Asia and was demanding a new cost-sharing deal, the United States was pressing for more Australian troops for Vietnam. In February, 1966, British Defense Minister Denis Healey visited Canberra to confer with the Australian and New Zealand governments about defense problems in the region. In a public address and in answer to questions he said that Britain had no intentions of "ratting on any of its existing commitments," but the current review was really concerned with the next twenty-five years. Britain intended to remain, in the military sense, a world power. "We intend to maintain a world influence." But his government had come to the conclusion that so far as any major military operations outside of Europe were concerned, "we can only plan to undertake them as part of a collective force." The best defense was a sound economy, and this called for a fair sharing of the burden. "No alliance can survive if one country is asked to bear a share of the common burden which is totally out of proportion to its national resources as compared with those of others." In proportion to her wealth, the United Kingdom was spending more money on forces abroad than any other country.[30]

[28] A consideration on the part of Britain may well have been the debt of honor it owed Australia and New Zealand for their generous support in the two World Wars.

[29] There are influential Australians who are very critical of the government for not spending more on defense. Donald Horne, former editor of the Sydney *Observer* and the *Bulletin*, in his recent book, *The Lucky Country: Australia in the Sixties* (Ringwood, 1964), 170, observes that "Australia has been spending about 3 percent of its national income on defence (the smallest of any advanced economy in the world); Canada spends 5.5 percent, the United States, 11.3 percent. Australia could give itself a coherent minimum defence force and still spend less than Canada."

[30] *The Age*, Feb. 3, 1966.

Healey was asked if Britain was planning to abandon its Singapore base, and if so, if it had plans for building a base in Australia. He replied that it made no "military sense at all" for Britain to leave Singapore unless it was forced to, but if the Singapore government should withdraw its support and there was no place else to go, "then we shall have to go home." The British presence in Singapore gave Britain "immense advantages which she would not enjoy if she had to leave the area." When asked if Britain were offered a site for a base in Australia would it accept, he replied, "We do intend to maintain a military capability in this part of the world. Where alternative sites to Singapore and Malaysia would be sited is a question for common discussion."[31]

Despite the British defense minister's assurances, Australia still was anxious about British intentions. In May it still was seeking more definite statements from the British government that there would be no change in British defense commitments east of Suez, and London was reminded that Australia was proceeding with her defense program on the basis of reassurances of continued support from Britain.[32] The cause of Australia's concern was the Indonesian-Malaysian rapprochement and new pressures within the Labor party against the Wilson government's Asian policy. On June 1, Wilson gave renewed assurances.[33]

[31] *The Age*, Feb. 3, 1966. In reply to a statement that in the talk of a common approach and a common action in Southeast Asia, Britain remained the odd man out in Vietnam, he said, "You might as well say that America remains the odd man out in Malaysia." It was "recognized in Washington that the task we are performing south of Vietnam is of interest to the West as a whole." In response to a question Wilson declared in Parliament that if Britain's position in Singapore became untenable, it might be necessary to withdraw to Australia and "discussions on that point had already occurred." *The Times* (London), July 13, 1966.

[32] *The New York Times*, June 1, 1966.

[33] *The New York Times*, June 2, 1966. At a closed meeting of the Labor members of Parliament on June 15, Wilson decisively defeated a motion calling for the withdrawal of all British forces from Malaysia, Singapore, and the Persian Gulf area by 1969-1970. The vote was 225 to 54. *Ibid.*, June 16, 1966.

But eleven months later the British government announced a "firm decision" to accelerate troop withdrawals from the Far East. Healey stated the number of British civilians and troops would be reduced by 20,000 by April, 1968, and further reductions would be made after that. At the time of the announcement (May 1, 1967) there were about 50,000 British troops and about 25,000 civilians in the Singapore-Malaysia area.[34] In another decade there will be few, if any, British troops in the Far East. Apparently Wilson and Healey were persuaded by their economic colleagues that the British economy and balance of payments position left no alternative. The British leaders now seem reconciled to resigning pretensions to world power status.

It may be assumed that both Australia and the United States are unhappy about the British plans—Australia because it means a further weakening of British ties and the loss of a moderating influence in its relations with Washington, and the United States because it is eager for the company of old friends in its troubles in Vietnam and Southeast Asia and because the British can play a stabilizing role in Malaya, Singapore, and elsewhere. Another point of view, expressed in a scholarly journal, is that the continued British military presence in the Pacific was "likely to complicate Australia's relations with South-East Asia in a way which the American presence did not—or—the British presence would probably succeed in estranging most states not already estranged by the American presence."[35] The British military withdrawal from Southeast Asia will tend to make Australians more conscious than ever of their dependence on the United States for security, but it will also tend to give Washington a deeper appreciation for Australian support and cooperation in the Pacific.

[34] *The New York Times,* May 2, 1967.
[35] G. St. J. Barclay, "Problems of Australian Foreign Policy, January to June, 1960," *Australian Journal of Politics and History,* Dec. 1966.

Pressed by current events, Australian views on national security have undergone profound change in the last two decades. Occasionally, however, some of the earlier, naive ideas still are evident. Should northern Australia be developed? The next significant threat of aggression is likely to come there. If this area should be invaded while still undeveloped, would there be any world sentiment for risking a war to repel such occupation?[36] On the other hand, if it were developed it might attract hostile occupation. Some greet the idea of a British base on Australian territory with little enthusiasm; as late as mid-1965 an important metropolitan daily argued editorially, "How would it suit Australia to have a massive British base established there [Darwin]? At first sight there is the picture of a greater Darwin and the quicker development of the Northern Territory arising from such a move. But does Australia really want to create an image in Asia of being the last bastion of British power in the Pacific? . . . Australia needs to consider carefully before undertaking military commitments which will identify her as an outpost of European colonial power and jeopardize her chances of friendly association in the Asian sphere."[37]

More and more, as the 1966 elections indicated, Australians are seeing their defense problem as it is outlined by Hasluck:

For the foreseeable future, the presence of non-Asian strength in the area, and particularly the strength of the United States, will be essential if fear is to be removed and freedom of choice restored. The countries of the region are entitled to look outside their borders for "foreign" help. Self-governing nations are entitled to decide whether and to what extent they will prepare the bases from which a concerted resistance to aggression will be maintained. The reality that has to be faced is that at present no balance to the power of China can be found in southern Asia.

36 See *Canberra Times*, Feb. 16, 1966.
37 *Adelaide News*, Aug. 11, 1965.

The balance has to be provided from outside Asia, and unless it is provided the region will fall under the domination of the Communist regime of Peking.[38]

With China's rapid development of an arsenal of nuclear weapons the views of the Australian government leaders will become more popular. So also will the British plan for an integrated defense system involving Australia, New Zealand, the United Kingdom, and the United States. Britain will have to be induced (for which it is probably already prepared) to extend its commitments into the Indian Ocean.[39] There is the temptation for Australia to develop its own nuclear deterrent, but this would mean a wasteful diversion of resources, and it is not likely that Australia will attempt this. Almost certainly, though, it will become more directly involved in nuclear defense. Also, Australia will become more dependent upon the United States for security. In its search for security Australia would seem to have to choose between allying itself with a great power or arming itself sufficiently to become a garrison state.

[38] "Australia and Southeast Asia," *Foreign Affairs*, XLIII, 61.

[39] The British government announced on July 18, 1967, that it planned to reduce by half its military forces in Singapore and Malaya by 1970-1971 and to withdraw the remainder by the mid-1970's. The possibility of "using facilities in Australia and of making a new staging airfield in the British Indian Ocean territory" was being examined. SEATO, Malaysia, and the Commonwealth were informed that "we intend to change our Far East commitments." Britain had 37,300 troops, 4,400 naval personnel, and 10,100 air force men in the Far East. *The New York Times*, July 19, 1967.

8 *Australia's Future in Asia*

Before we start debating what we are doing or what we ought to do in Australian foreign policy let us face plainly the fact that there are two things we cannot do. We cannot change Australia's geographical situation and we cannot cancel out the great forces that are bringing massive changes in the world today and particularly in the southern half of Asia. We in Australia are living on the edge of a great upheaval both in human relations and in the ideas which influence the conduct of mankind. We cannot withdraw from this region and we cannot do anything to prevent the upheaval.

> PAUL HASLUCK
> Minister for External Affairs
> House of Representatives
> March 10, 1966

Australia is sinking into the Pacific and a new state is rising which we might call Austerica.

> C. L. SULZBERGER
> *The New York Times*
> March 25, 1966

IF AUSTRALIA HAS not quite succeeded in solving the main problem of its foreign policy—reconciling its history with its geography—it has gone some distance toward meeting the problem of its security. In doing so it has departed markedly from its traditions, but it has not succeeded in winning acceptance by Asians as an Asian country, albeit white. Again it feels threatened by Asia, but now by a huge Communist country with rapidly increasing military power. Australia has not been able to establish close friendly relations with its Asian neighbors, chiefly because of the great social upheaval which these nations are undergoing.[1]

Frequently it is said that the discrimination against Asian immigrants hangs like a millstone around the necks of Australian diplomats in Asian countries. In this policy Australia's geographical isolation from the West and its historical isolation from the East are emphasized clearly. Australia's admission of Asian immigrants was restricted severely by an act of 1901, which prohibited entry of persons who failed to pass a "dictation test" in a European language. This device was abolished in 1958. In addition to the differential admission policy, Asians were subjected to discrimination in the period of residence required for citizenship. For Europeans the requirement was five years, while for others, it was fifteen. A number of adjustments in immigration policy have been made since World War II, such as the free admission of the spouse, whether man or woman, of an Australian citizen; the extension of the rights of citizenship to numerous Asians who took refuge in Australia during the war; and

[1] Part of the difficulty undoubtedly is with the Australians. They have not found it easy to orient themselves to the new power situation in Asia. They have "not gained a 'real feel' for the part of the world they live in, even if many of them now talk about it. . . . Australians talk of Asia as if they lived in Europe." Donald Horne, *The Lucky Country: Australia in the Sixties* (Ringwood, 1964), 82.

the extension of citizenship to many Asian residents of Papua and New Guinea. In March, 1966, a further liberalization was announced, and the residence requirement for citizenship for Asians was reduced to five years, the same as for Europeans. Furthermore, certain classes of Asians would be admitted more freely, chiefly persons with specialized technical skills and with high attainments in the arts and sciences.[2] While significant, these modifications do not efface the contrast between sharply restricted immigration from Asia and promoted, assisted immigration from Europe.

Australians are reexamining their "white" immigration policy. The motives behind the policy are obvious—fear of competition and the desire for a homogeneous, unified population. White Australians are not yet ready to admit Asians on the same basis as Europeans, although they are becoming sensitive to criticism of their discriminatory policy and are prepared for some liberalization. They would like to have the term "white Australia policy" forgotten. After more than fifty years of use, the term was dropped by the supreme governing body of the Labor party in 1965 from its statement of policy, but the party's position on the matter remained basically unchanged. The Australian Council of Churches in January, 1966, asked the minister of immigration to increase substantially the number of non-Europeans granted permanent residence in Australia each year.[3] Other organizations called for reforms in immigration policy.[4] Leaders in the business community are expressing doubts about the policy and the way it is administered. In an article under the caption "High Cost of White Australia," *The Aus-*

[2] There are about 40,000 non-Europeans living in Australia, of whom about 17,000 are citizens.

[3] *West Australian*, Jan. 28, 1966. A similar request was made a year earlier.

[4] *Canberra Times*, Feb. 2, 1966. After a poll of its members the Australian Association for Cultural Freedom issued a statement saying that there was "every sign" that the Australian people were "ready for immigration reform." *Ibid.*, Feb. 19, 1966.

tralian Financial Review[5] declared that the economic implications of "white Australia" "are beginning to highlight the
ultimate sterility of this policy," that unless changes are
made Australia "will never achieve its ambition of being an
influential industrial power in the Pacific." Moreover, it concluded, "Australia may find it difficult to enter close alliances
with nations which, with good reason, regard it as advocating
a kind of international apartheid."

In the speech in which he announced the liberalization of
the immigration regulations, Holt explained why the government was reviewing the restrictive aspects of its policy.
An examination was desirable, he said, because of "Australia's increasing involvement in Asian development, the
rapid growth of our trade with Asian countries, our participation on a large scale in an increasing number of aid
projects in the area, the considerable number of Asian
students—now well over 12,000—receiving education in
Australia, the expansion of our military efforts and the scale
of diplomatic contact, the growth of tourism to and from
the countries of Asia."[6]

While Australians are ready to relax their immigration
regulations to some extent, they are not prepared to change
the policy basically. They are convinced that it is justifiable
and that they can explain it to the satisfaction of their Asian
neighbors. They point out that the policy is not racial, but
is designed to protect social unity and living standards, and
that every country reserves the right to determine the composition of its population. Holt claimed that from its unity
Australia derives strength and a community life free from
serious minority and racial problems. All countries of Southeast Asia maintain restrictions on immigration to serve their
own national policies, he continued.[7] Hasluck has said that
he does not think his country's restrictive policy is "a real

[5] Feb. 7, 1966.
[6] *Canberra Times,* March 9, 1966.
[7] *Canberra Times,* March 9, 1966.

barrier to confidence and understanding between us and Asian countries."[8] However that may be, individual cases of harsh rejections and expulsions cause bitter reactions, and the Australian government undoubtedly is anxious to avoid these incidents.

IN THE LAST QUARTER of a century a remarkably close relationship between Australia and the United States has developed. The frequent visits of the leaders of the Australian government to Washington and the visits of Secretary Rusk and Vice President Humphrey, and especially the visit of President Johnson to Australia during the 1966 election campaign, are evidences of this growing closeness. It may be argued that this is the result of the situation in Vietnam, and therefore, may be only temporary. But behind Vietnam stands China, and whatever the outcome in Vietnam, China will long remain the central problem of Asian foreign policy.

While there is much to draw the two countries together, there also are possibilities for friction. Australians naturally are sensitive to the "taint of satellitism," the "tinge of puppetry." Care will have to be exercised lest such feelings be allowed to develop. The Labor opposition is likely to charge the government with having no foreign policy of its own,

[8] As a press conference in New York, April, 1966, in reply to a question whether the role Australia seeks to fill in Asia might not be inhibited by the "white Australia" policy, *Current Notes*, XXXVII, 234. An editorial in *Straits Times* (Singapore) supports Hasluck's views: "Australians, to their credit, worry much more about their country's immigration policies than do the Asians supposed to feel so mortally offended because they cannot go to live there. . . . Any country's immigration policy is its own affair." Quoted by *Canberra Times*, Feb. 24, 1965. But for a contrary point of view see Robin W. Winks in *Malaysia: A Survey*, ed. Wang Gungwin (New York, 1964), 390-91. Donald Horne sharply states a contrary view: Australia "encourages and subsidizes migration from Europe, including the migration of those who do not speak English, yet it conducts such rigorous (and secret) tests against Asians that very few Asians get in. This is taken to be racialist by Asians, and so it is, in effect, whatever its motives. It causes Australia to be distrusted by every nation in Asia." *The Lucky Country*, 102.

following "a kind of hitch-hiking diplomacy." The large and growing American investments in Australia already have caused a mounting pressure for greater local participation in foreign business ventures in the country. Trade relations between the two countries are subject to difficulties, because many Australians and Americans are engaged in similar lines of business and both countries follow strongly protectionist policies. Though its wool is superior to American wool, Australia has difficulty in getting into the American market because of high tariff duties. Imports of Australian meat, lead, and zinc are limited strictly by quotas, and Australian dairy products are virtually excluded from the American market.[9]

There is also the disturbing doubt on the part of some Australians, even those who are convinced that only the presence of the United States prevents China from overrunning the Asian mainland, whether or not the United States would use its power in Australian interests in Asian conflicts that were not associated with the containment of Communist China. They have not forgotten that in the West Irian conflict Australia and the Netherlands received no support from Washington, and as a result Australia "had to throw in its hand."[10]

A COUNTRY WHICH comprises one-fourth of the human race is an important factor in world politics, whatever its policies may be. How to come to terms with Communist China is probably the most important international problem of this generation. This is especially true for its neighbors. Most Australians are worried about China, and because of their

[9] In 1964, Australia charged the United States with virtually repudiating a trade agreement by enacting a law setting up a complex quota system for meat imports, as a result of which the Australian quota was reduced. Australian exporters estimated their trade loss at $A40 million annually.

[10] See Donald Horne, *The Lucky Country*, 91-92.

geographic position, this is for them no remote, academic matter.[11] While the Australian commercial interests fear the threat of Chinese Communism, they are attracted by the vast possibilities of the Chinese market. Australia has found in Red China an important outlet for its wheat; more than ten million tons of the cereal were sold to Peking between 1960 and 1965. The chief beneficiaries of this trade, the wheat farmers, are nearly all members of the Country party and thus are supporters of the government's anti-Communist China policy.

In its policy toward China, Australia has departed markedly from that followed by Britain. It has not recognized the Communist regime and it has opposed the seating of Peking in the seat of China in the organs of the United Nations. However, Australia did not immediately enter into diplomatic relations with Nationalist China and did not open an embassy in Taipei until 1965. Hasluck explained in Parliament that the reasons for this delay were "connected mainly with the difficulties of maintaining a rapidly expanding service and of staffing all the posts that we would like to staff."[12] He assured the House that "our relations with China are close and friendly, and they are, I believe, harmonious." Nationalist China did have a diplomatic representative in Canberra and there were frequent exchange visits between the two capitals on the cabinet level.

Australia has its own policy toward Communist China. While it is similar to that of the United States, it is not as rigid. With the exception of certain strategic items, trade is promoted. The government permits, if it does not encour-

[11] A very somber view of the situation is taken by Donald Horne. He sees the possibility of Chinese dominance stretching over the future of Asia. "It does so whether China remains with its present ideology or not. To Australia China is a much greater reality than it is to any of the countries of Western Europe. Even to America China is not a final problem. It is the other half of a final problem. Chinese-Communist victories in South-East Asia could mean a threat to Australian sovereignty or its collapse. But the rest of the world could survive." *The Lucky Country*, 101.

[12] Aug. 17, 1965, *Current Notes*, XXXVI, 510.

age, exchange visits by cultural and scientific representatives. "The basic problem," says Holt,[13] "is how to live with mainland China and finding a way for it to fit into the international community. We consider we should do what we can to bring about changes in attitudes, policies and conditions and thus in the relationships between China and neighboring countries and other great powers. At the same time, it must be made clear to Communist China what are the limits beyond which policies can not be forced by one nation in disregard of another. We are constantly on the watch for the constructive opportunities change may bring."

Hasluck told Parliament that his government was willing to explore new ways of living with Communist China, that it would even consider entering into diplomatic relations with it, but that Peking had imposed unacceptable conditions by insisting that Australia acknowledge Communist China's sovereignty over Taiwan. "Could any Australian Government," he asked, "accept the argument that a political entity of nearly 13 million people should be sacrificed to satisfy the imagined interests of another?" Relations with Communist China were under a strain; Australia should not aggravate it "by trying to force openings that are firmly closed against us," he said.[14]

THOUGH IT IS THE second most populous state in the world, India is rarely mentioned in any discussion of the power politics of Southeast Asia. Yet, like China, India borders on the region and for a considerable period also made an important cultural impact on it. Because of the presence of some two million Indians in the area, India could claim an important interest in it and find grounds for exerting pressure on the politics of at least those countries in which the Indians

[13] In answer to question of the editor of the *Straits Times* (Singapore), Oct. 31, 1966, *Current Notes*, XXXVII, 675.
[14] *The New York Times*, Aug. 19, 1966.

are concentrated—Burma, Malaysia, and Singapore. Yet, because of its neutralist attitude and probably also because of its many problems at home, India has concerned itself little with the region. India sought to win the moral leadership of Asia but failed in this, and China's growing military strength further weakened India's prestige.

India gave Indonesia valuable support in its struggle for independence. It convened an Asian Conference, in which Australia was the only non-Asian country to participate. This conference asked the United Nations Security Council to intervene in Indonesia after the Dutch took their second police action. For a few years relations between India and Indonesia were cordial, marked by exchanges of official visits by Prime Minister Nehru and President Sukarno, but relations between the two governments cooled. Sukarno was disappointed in the meager support Indonesia received from India in its struggle with the Dutch for West New Guinea. By 1965, Indo-Indonesian relations had deteriorated so much that Indonesia not only gave Pakistan full moral support in its conflict with India, but it even offered it military assistance. Relations improved after the military takeover in Djakarta; India gave Indonesia a credit of Rs100 million.

If China continues its pressure upon India and cultivates Pakistan, India may shed its neutralism and seek Asian help. Little economic and military help can be found there, but Asian moral support is very important for ideological purposes. Thus, continued pressure by the Chinese may well have the effect of building closer ties between India and Indonesia, Malaysia, Thailand, and even Australia.[15]

TRADE BETWEEN Australia and Japan has increased enormously. Japan is greatly interested in increasing its trade

[15] See D. P. Singhal, "Indian Policy in South-East Asia," *Australian Journal of Politics and History*, XII, 258-70.

with Southeast Asia. The region now absorbs about 30 percent of its exports, but this trade is increasing less rapidly than Japan's overall trade. Until the region is economically developed its trade can increase very little, hence Japan is eager to provide technical and economic assistance to the countries of the area. Australia is likewise interested in the economic development of the region, and hence the two countries are working closely on bilateral and multilateral plans for regional cooperation.[16]

Closer cultural relations are certain to follow these commercial relations. Japan will not be swayed from its policy of keeping aloof from active participation in power politics, but it has taken an initial step. It joined with eight other countries in forming the Asian and Pacific Council (ASPAC), which held its first meeting in June, 1966, at Seoul, Korea. The council members unanimously affirmed their support of South Vietnam in its fight against "external aggression and subversion" and invited other countries in the Asian and Pacific region to join in the common determination of the group to "preserve their integrity and sovereignty in the face of external threats."[17] Members of the Pacific Council are South Korea, Australia, Nationalist China, Japan, Malaysia, New Zealand, the Philippines, Thailand, and South Vietnam. Laos attended as an observer, and Indonesia expressed an interest in joining the group. The head of New Zealand's delegation, Minister of Customs Norman L. Shelton, stated that the conference was "a long step forward" in bringing New Zealand and Australia into partnership with Asian countries. Significantly, through the formation of the council Australia and New Zealand have been brought into a political association with Japan.

[16] See Denis Warner, "First Steps Toward an Asian Common Market," *The Reporter*, May 18, 1967. One of the objectives of an Australian-Japanese Business Cooperation Committee is the establishment of a Pacific Basin plan for economic development and cooperation.

[17] *The New York Times*, June 6, 1966.

PAPUA AND THE Trust Territory of New Guinea present a difficult problem for Australia. Regardless of the advances in armaments and the changes in warfare, New Guinea will remain important for Australia's security. At its nearest point the island is only one hundred miles from the Australian mainland. The security problem is tied up with the political, however. The fervently anticolonial members of the United Nations are prodding Australia to grant independence to the two territories at an early date. New Guinea's jungle terrain is one of the most rugged in the world. The territories' sparse population is divided into numerous primitive ethnological groups with hundreds of different languages, living in mountain pockets with great distances between them. To build a nation, much less a strong society, out of such groups and under such geographic conditions is a slow process.

To grant self-government prematurely would be unwise and would not benefit the inhabitants. An independent Papua would be weak, and its national existence would be precarious. The policy of the Australian government has been to proceed slowly in building a stable democratic government in which the 25,000 white settlers can cooperate with the 2,000,000 indigenous inhabitants.[18] Australia's aim in New Guinea was stated clearly by Sir Percy Spender in 1950 when he was minister of external affairs. It is, he said, to build up "a friendly, prosperous and loyal people who will be able in times of crisis to assist in the protection of their own interests and to provide strength, not weakness, to the Australian nation, to whom they must inevitably turn as their protector." He continued, "if we are to hold these territories safe from external aggression they must be de-

[18] The area of the Trust Territory is 93,000 square miles, including the Bismarck archipelago, and of Papua, 90,600. The area of West New Guinea (Indonesian West Irian) is 153,000 square miles.

veloped as quickly as our resources permit."[19] This has been the government's policy, under increasing pressure and with heightened tempo.

The anticolonial members of the United Nations are not the only ones that have goaded the Australian government about New Guinea. The Labor opposition also argued about the issue. When Menzies described the Dutch proposal to internationalize West New Guinea as "constructive," a member of the House asked him if it was the intention of the government to make a similar proposal to the United Nations about Papua.[20] A leading Labor member of Parliament criticized the government for being "slow and ineffectual" in putting the argument for self-determination for West New Guinea in the United Nations. The reason for this, he asserted, was the "protracted and patriarchal performance" of the minister of territories in the administration of Australia's own trust territory, in view of which the argument would scarcely have appeared genuine.[21]

Whatever the original views of the leaders of the Menzies government may have been about the ultimate status of Papua, they gradually accepted independence as the goal. They knew, however, that the inhabitants of New Guinea were still in a primitive state, and it would be a long time before they would be ready for self-government. In June,

[19] House of Representatives, June 1, 1950, *Current Notes*, XXI, 383. Holt, in an interview with editor-in-chief of the *Straits Times* (Singapore), on Oct. 31, 1966, stated that Australia's aim was to give the territory "an institutional framework for democratic government where none existed before. We want to see develop there an appropriate modern economy that will be diversified and strong, so that the people can exercise their right to choose their own future. And we want to build bases for friendship over a whole range of subjects that will stand firm whatever the nature of the ultimate association of the Territory with Australia." *Current Notes*, XXXVII, 675-84.
[20] *Commonwealth Parliamentary Debates*, House, XXXIII, 1446.
[21] E. G. Whitlam, April 10, 1962, *CPD*, House, XXXV, 1509. According to Whitlam, no Papuan had yet been trained to cast a vote, nor had a single one been given a vote. Education had been provided for only one child in five, and for a school population of over half a million, only about 1,600 were receiving secondary education and only three were receiving college training.

1960, Hasluck said that Papua and the trust territory of New Guinea would not be ready for independence for thirty years. On the next day, though, Menzies made a statement of a different tenor to the press, saying he supported the idea that if you are in doubt, you should leave sooner than later. He remarked sagely that he had seen enough in recent years "to satisfy me that even though some independence may have been premature, where . . . [it has] . . . been a little premature . . . [it has] . . . at least been achieved with good will." He refused to set a target date for the independence of the two territories, but a week later Hasluck announced target dates for various stages in educational, social, and economic advancement.[22]

Before this the government had moved slowly in preparing the Papuans for self-government. Hasluck was convinced that unless solid social and economic foundations were laid, self-government would be meaningless and easily could lead to disaster. As the Papuans were among the most primitive people on earth, a long period of preparation was necessary, but since 1960 a sense of urgency has pervaded Australian policy in the territories. Australian grants to the territories rose from $19,840,000 in 1955-1956 to $78,000,000 in 1966-1967. These grants constitute the main component in a budget of $134,000,000. Many more millions are spent in the territories by various Australian departments. In 1964 a central legislative body, called the House of Assembly and composed of sixty-four members, was established. Thirty-eight Melanesians were elected to membership in the embryonic legislature in the election held that year. A national consciousness is slowly emerging, but the Australian government resists pressure to set a target date for independence. It insists that the people of Papua and New Guinea have the right "to choose their own political future, in their

[22] See J. D. Legge, "Problems of Australian Foreign Policy, January to June, 1960," *Australian Journal of Politics and History*, VI, 139-52.

own way, in their own time" and free from "outside pressure
in doing so."²³

In view of the situation in Southeast Asia, the similarity
in background of Australia and New Zealand, and their many
common interests, a drive for closer relations between the
two countries would be a natural development. New Zealand was invited to join the Australian federation when it
was in the process of formation. The ANZAC agreement
of 1944, which provided for consultation between the two
countries for defense and foreign policy, contained clauses
suggesting "the development of commerce between Australia
and New Zealand" and cooperation in promoting their industrial advancement. While cooperation in foreign policy
and defense has grown, closer economic relations develop
very slowly. After two years of negotiation, the two governments on August 17, 1965, entered into a free-trade agreement which placed items, covering about 60 percent of the
total trade between them, on a duty-free basis.²⁴

Further progress in establishing closer trade relations, as
well as a common market, will not be achieved easily, chiefly
because the economies of the two countries compete, and
the agreement of 1965 contains significant safeguards and
limitations. But if Britain joins the European Economic
Community, Australia and New Zealand may feel it necessary to strengthen their economies and their trade position
by unified action and a common front against the outside
world.

The obstacles to a closer political association are even
greater. The peoples of the two countries, partly because of

²³ Minister of territories in House of Representatives, May 4, 1966,
Current Notes, XXXVII, 293. He was repeating what Menzies had said
several years earlier.
²⁴ *Ibid.*, XXXVI, 467-80. *The New York Times*, Dec. 6, 1966,

their insular positions, have developed somewhat distinctive national characters, and the differences in area and population create difficulties. On the one hand, Australia, with four times the population of New Zealand, would not want to enter a political union on the basis of equality, and on the other, New Zealand would not want to exchange its status as an independent state for that of a state in the Australian federation. Yet there are significant factors pressuring for union. If threats to the security of the two states continue, and especially if Australia and New Zealand should fear that the United States might withdraw from the area or that disagreement might develop between them and America concerning security policy, concerted action would be highly desirable. Already Australia and New Zealand are faced with the necessity of greatly increased military expenditures. To obtain the maximum strength from their efforts and to insure the least damage to their balance-of-payments position, these expenditures must be planned and coordinated. This would require extensive economic and defense planning and coordination, and once started, this movement might gain momentum.[25]

ASIDE FROM the question of how serious a threat China is to Southeast Asia, Indonesia is and will continue to be Australia's major diplomatic problem. Since October, 1965, when the army took charge of the Djakarta government, relations between the two countries have been amicable. However, the political situation in Indonesia is not yet clear. The army has succeeded in stripping Sukarno of political power, but Sukarnoism—that strange hodgepodge of ideologies—will continue for some time as a disturbing force.

[25] See the excellent study, A. D. Robinson, *Towards a Tasman Community* (Wellington, 1965).

Furthermore, the military regime has the nearly impossible task of restoring the country's shattered economy and of coping with its desperate financial condition. Unless a massive, sustained program is undertaken, serious social unrest will appear, inspiring political results that cannot be predicted.

There are at least three spots where trouble between Australia and Indonesia might develop. If Indonesia, following the example of India concerning Goa, should forcibly occupy Portuguese Timor, the resulting situation would be problematic for Australia. If Indonesia was unopposed, it might be encouraged to attempt other conquests, perhaps in New Guinea, which is another sensitive area. Australia, however, would not want to incur the lasting hostility of its populous northern neighbor over this small area, nor the jeers of Africans and Asians as a defender of colonialism. Trouble easily could develop over New Guinea because of its peculiar situation.[26] The failure of Indonesia to hold a plebiscite in accordance with the agreement with the Netherlands, which resulted in the transfer of the territory to Indonesia, would bring an unfavorable response from Australia. Should the people of West Irian desire union with their eastern neighbors in the island, or should Indonesia attempt infiltration and subversion in the eastern half, serious tensions between the two countries undoubtedly would develop.

Nor is the situation in Malaysia free from possible trouble. The change of government in Djakarta has not solved Malaysia's racial problems, and Singapore and the federation are moving further apart. Conceivably, the Malays and the Indonesians might seek to solve the Chinese and Singapore problems by forming some kind of political union.

[26] See Chapter 4. The two countries are cooperating in demarking the boundary between West Irian and the territories of Papua and New Guinea.

Singapore's prime minister, Lee Kuan Yew, has expressed fear of such a possibility.[27] Or Singapore might attempt to solve its problem by moving closer to Indonesia. The situation is far from an equilibrium among the contending parties.

AUSTRALIA has attempted diligently to be a good neighbor to Indonesia. It has been generous with economic aid, and there were 203 Indonesian students in Australia under the Colombo Plan in 1964. At the time 160 other Indonesians were studying in Australia. Australians also have studied in Indonesia, and the two peoples are getting to know each other. Private individual Australians also have provided Indonesia with technical assistance. The Australian Volunteer Graduate Association Scheme for Indonesia has financed the sending of a considerable number of young Australians to Indonesia to build "bridges for friendship."[28]

Australians are aware of the difficulties they, as a European people residing in close contact with Asian peoples, must overcome in insuring "our own comprehension of our neighbors," of explaining "ourselves to them," and of having "ourselves understood by them." They have made some progress, but, as a former minister of external affairs concluded, "It remains a continuing task in which we need sensitive and skillful diplomacy."[29]

[27] He is quoted as having said, "Our long term survival demands there is no government in Malaysia that goes with Indonesia. Life would be very difficult if I found myself between Malaysia and Indonesia." *The Observer,* Aug. 15, 1965.

[28] See Ivan Southall, *Indonesia Face to Face* (Singapore).

[29] Sir Garfield Barwick, Address to the Australian Institute of Political Science, Jan. 25, 1964, *Current Notes,* XXXV, 10-11.

BIBLIOGRAPHY

Albinski, Henry E. *Australia and the China Problem during the Korean War*, Canberra, 1964.

Aughterson, W. V., ed. *Taking Stock: Aspects of Mid-Century Life in Australia*, Melbourne, 1953.

Members of the Australian Institute of International Affairs. *Australia and the Pacific*, Princeton, 1944.

Bailey, Kenneth Hamilton. *Australia*, Berkeley, 1947.

Cairns, J. F. *Living With Asia*, London and Melbourne, 1965.

Casey, R. G. *Friends and Neighbors: Australia and the World*, Melbourne, 1954.

Churchill, Winston. *The Second World War*, 4 vols., Boston, 1950.

Coleman, Peter and others. *Forces in Australian Politics*, Melbourne, 1963.

Commonwealth Parliamentary Debates, Canberra, 1901–.

Consulate General of the Republic of Indonesia. *News and Views*, New York, various issues.

Crisp, L. F. *The Australian Federal Labor Party, 1901-1951*, London, 1955.

Crisp, L. F. *Australian National Government*, Croydon, 1965.

Davies, A. F. and Encel, S. *Australian Society: A Sociological Introduction*, Melbourne, 1965.

Department of External Affairs. *Current Notes*, Canberra, 1929–.

Downer, A. D. *The Influence of Migration on Australian Foreign Policy*, Roy Milne Lecture, Australian Institute of International Affairs, Melbourne, 1960.

Eggleston, F. W. *Reflections on Australian Foreign Policy*, Melbourne, 1957.

Embassy of Indonesia, Information Division, Washington. *A Survey of the Controversial Problem of the Establishment of the Federation of Malaysia*, Washington, no date.

Evatt, Herbert Vere. *Australia in World Affairs*, Sydney, 1946.

Evatt, Herbert Vere. *Foreign Policy of Australia: Speeches*, Sydney and London, 1945.

Grant, Bruce. *Indonesia*, Melbourne, 1964.

Gratton, C. Hartley, ed. *Australia*, Berkeley, 1947.

Greenwood, Gordon and Harper, Norman, eds. *Australia in World Affairs, 1950-1955*, Melbourne, 1957.

Greenwood, Gordon and Harper, Norman, eds. *Australia in World Affairs, 1956-1960*, Melbourne, 1963.

Gungwin, Wang, ed. *Malaysia: A Survey*, New York, 1964.

Hancock, W. K. *Australia*, London, 1930.

Horne, Donald. *The Lucky Country: Australia in the Sixties*, Ringwood, 1964.

Levi, Werner. *Australia's Outlook on Asia*, East Lansing, 1958.

Lijphart, Arend. *The Trauma of Decolonization: The Dutch and West New Guinea*, New Haven, 1966.

Millar, T. B. *Australia's Defence*, Melbourne, 1965.

Overacker, Louise. *The Australian Party System*, New Haven, 1952.

Parkinson, C. Northcote. *Britain in the Far East: The Singapore Naval Base*, Singapore, 1955.

Robinson, A. D. *Towards a Tasman Community*, Wellington, 1965.

Rosecrance, N. *Australian Diplomacy and Japan, 1945-1951*, Melbourne, 1962.

Report by a Study Group of the Royal Institute of International Affairs. *Collective Defence in South East Asia—The Manila Treaty and Its Implications*, London, 1956.

Schlesinger, Jr., Arthur N. *A Thousand Days: John F. Kennedy in the White House*, Boston, 1965.

Souter, Gavin. *New Guinea: The Last Unknown*, New York, 1966.

Southall, Ivan. *Indonesia Face to Face*, Singapore, no date.

Subcommittee of Pacific Bases of the Committee on Naval Affairs, House of Representatives, 79th Congress, 1st Session, Aug. 1945. *Study of Pacific Bases*, Washington, 1945.

Tilby, A. Wyatt. *Australia, 1688-1911*, Boston, 1912.

United Nations General Assembly. *Official Records*, New York, 1945—.

United Nations Security Council. *Official Records*, New York, 1945—.

INDEX

ANZAC Agreement: 134, 165; negotiated, 21-23; parliamentary debate
on, 23-25
ANZAM Agreement, 86, 146
ANZUS Treaty: 126; scope of, 98-
100; negotiation of, 136-39
Australia: changed international position, 2; British orientation of, 3-4;
foreign trade, 6-7; changing economy of, 7; change to decimal currency system in, 7n; population
growth in, 7-8; concern for national security, 9; as middle power,
10; decentralization of life in, 15-
16; constitutional system of, 15-17;
interest in islands to north, 19-
20; and Indonesian independence
movement, 33-37; and West New
Guinea dispute, 41-77; and defense and West New Guinea, 46,
52; and alleged policy shift over
West New Guinea, 53-58; and
dilemma in West New Guinea
dispute, 56-57; and West New
Guinea policy shift, 69-70; and
frustration over West New Guinea, 73-74, 74n; West New Guinea
policy summarized, 76-77; stake
in Southeast Asia, 78; and defense of Malaya, 79-86; supports
Malaysia, 92; ambivalent relations with Indonesia, 96-97, 102-
103, 105, 107; China policy, 109;
support of U.S. policy in Vietnam, 114-19; defense problem,
130-31; interest in plans for
regional defense, 134-35; pre-
World War II defense policy, 133;
attitude toward U.S. treaty with
Japan, 136; military buildup after
1964, 139-40; defense partnership
with U.S., 142-43; foreign economic aid and technical assistance
policy, 143; and India, 158-59;
and Japan, 160-61; importance of

Australia *(continued):*
relations with Indonesia, 166-67;
development of close relations with
U.S., 156-57; policy toward Communist China, 158-59; relations
with New Zealand, 165-66
Australian Federation movement, 11
Australian-Netherlands Joint Statement of Cooperation, 49-50, 51, 77
Azahari, A. M., 89

Barwick, Sir Garfield: on Australia's
place in world, 10; on West New
Guinea dispute, 65-66, 69-70; on
Australia's interest in West New
Guinea dispute, 72-73; on alleged
military arrangement with the Neth-
erlands, 73; on Malaysia and
Southeast Asia's stability, 91; on
Australia's military commitment to
Malaysia, 91; and efforts at media-
tion in Indonesian-Malaysian con-
flict, 91; on U.S. support of Aus-
tralia in Malaysian confrontation,
98-100; announces Australian aid
to Vietnam, 109-10; on Asia and
Australian defense, 130; on North
West Cape Agreement with U.S.,
140; on nuclear-free zone, 140; on
SEATO's value, 144-45
Brunei, revolt, 89

Calwell, A. A.: anti-American position, 15; and U.S. nuclear bases in
Australia, 17n; and Manus Island
debate, 28; on Australian interest
in West New Guinea dispute, 44;
on regional pact idea, 61; on West
New Guinea policy, 67-68, 70; on
sending troops to Malaya, 84; on
creation of Malaysia, 93; on defense treaty with Malaysia, 95; on
U.S. ANZAC commitment, 98; attacks decision to send troops to
South Vietnam, 112-13; attacks

Calwell *(continued)*:
government policy on Vietnam, 119-20; demands withdrawal of conscripts in Vietnam, 129
Casey, Lord Richard G.: 137, 144; on perils to Australia, 2; appointed governor general, 12; attitude on Manus Island base negotiations, 30-31; denies existence of Dutch-Australian military alliance, 50; cautions Indonesia, 51; on regional pact idea, 53; and alleged West New Guinea policy shift, 53-57; on West New Guinea and Australian defense, 74; on Malayan "Emergency," 85; on U.S. treaty with Japan, 136
Chifley, J. B.: and new direction of Australia's foreign policy, 5; views on Indonesian independence movement, 33, 34
China, Communist: Australian policy toward, 109; and Southeast Asia, 150-51; Australian concern over threat, 157-59
Churchill, Winston, 132
Cobbold Commission, 90
Commonwealth, British: Australian attachment to, 4; and Indonesian-Malaysian dispute, 100-101
Curtin, John: and new direction of Australia's foreign policy, 4-5; views on ANZAC Agreement, 26; on Australian dependence on U.S., 132; on importance of Singapore for Australian defense, 132-33

Defense: emerging policy, 131-51; Australian attitudes toward British base in Australia, 149; changing Australian attitudes on, 149-50. *See also* Barwick, Sir Garfield; Calwell, A. A.; Casey, Lord Richard G.; Curtin, John; Evatt, Herbert Vere; Hasluck, Paul; Holt, Harold; Menzies, Robert; Spender, Sir Percy
De Quay, J. E., 61, 65, 71
Douglas-Home, Sir Alec, 6

Evatt, Herbert Vere: and reorientation of Australia's foreign policy, 5; on Australia's international status, 18; and ANZAC Agreement, 18, 20-27; develops active foreign policy, 19; and negotiations with U.S. on Manus Island base, 27-33; views on his conduct of Australian foreign policy, 37-39; on regional pact idea, 47, 53, 134-35; on West New Guinea dispute, 43-44, 56, 75; on West New Guinea and United Nations, 45, 53; criticizes Casey's policy on West New Guinea, 52-54; on Malaya, 84-85, 86
External Affairs, Department of, 12

Far East Strategic Reserve, 92
Great Britain. *See* United Kingdom

Hasluck, Paul: comments on Evatt and ANZAC Agreement, 25-26, 38n; visits Djakarta, 107; on U.S. bombing of North Vietnam, 116-17; on Australia's SEATO obligations in Vietnam, 121-22; on Australia's stake in Vietnam, 128; on scope of ANZUS, 138-39; on SEATO's value, 145n; views on national defense, 150-51; on problem of Australian foreign policy, 152; on relations with Communist China, 158-59; on self-government for Trust Territory and Papua, 164
Healey, Denis, 147-49
Holt, Harold: on Empire ties, 13; criticizes ANZAC Agreement, 24; on further aid for Vietnam, 119; on following U.S. policies in Vietnam, 118-19; on Australian aims in Vietnam, 120-21; on Vietnam policy, 127-28; becomes prime minister, 127; on SEATO's value, 144; on immigration policy, 155-56; on Australia's aims in Trust Territory of New Guinea, 163n

Immigration policy: in early years, 3; effect on national character, 8-9;

www.ingramcontent.com/pod-product-compliance
Lightning Source LLC
Chambersburg PA
CBHW031444280326
41927CB00037B/302